Modern Critical Interpretations

William Shakespeare's Coriolanus

Modern Critical Interpretations

These and other titles in preparation

Modern Critical Interpretations

William Shakespeare's
Coriolanus

Edited and with an introduction by

Harold Bloom
Sterling Professor of the Humanities
Yale University

Chelsea House Publishers ◇ *1988*

NEW YORK ◇ NEW HAVEN ◇ PHILADELPHIA

Printed and bound in the United States of America

10 9 8 7 6 5 4 3 2 1

∞ The paper used in this publication meets the minimum
requirements of the American National Standard for Permanence
of Paper for Printed Library Materials, Z39.48-1984.

Library of Congress Cataloging-in-Publication Data

William Shakespeare's Coriolanus.

   (Modern critical interpretations)
   Bibliography: p.
   Includes index.
   1. Shakespeare, William, 1564–1616.   Coriolanus.
I. Bloom, Harold.   II. Series.
PR2805.W54   1988   822.3'3   87-8094
ISBN 0-87754-923-0 (alk. paper)

Contents

Editor's Note

This book gathers together a representative selection of the best modern criticism of Shakespeare's tragedy *Coriolanus*. The critical essays are reprinted here in the chronological order of their original publication. I am grateful to John Rogers for his aid in editing this volume.

My introduction builds upon Hazlitt's analysis of *Coriolanus* as an instance of the close association between poetry and power. Eugene M. Waith begins the chronological sequence with his classic discussion of *Coriolanus* as heroic tragedy, with the Roman general as a grand instance of "the Herculean hero." In Kenneth Burke's equally classic essay, the play is viewed as a "grotesque" tragedy, so that the function of Coriolanus is to be "a master of vituperation," who is then tragically victimized so as to perform a ritualistic catharsis for his society.

The way in which the hero's virtue is also his vice, a frequent design in Shakespeare's tragedies, is studied in *Coriolanus* by Norman Rabkin. Imagery of hunger and feeding in the play is brilliantly related in Janet Adelman's essay to the dialectical interplay of dependency and aggression between Coriolanus and Volumnia. A. D. Nuttall, in an illuminating excursus, shows us the kind of Rome and the kinds of Romans Shakespeare created for this play. The philosopher Stanley Cavell, expounding interpretive problems of poetry and politics, essentially unveils religious analogues in *Coriolanus*. Perhaps finding a more benign totality in the play than most critics have done, Anne Barton concludes this volume by seeing *Coriolanus* as a tragedy that is primarily a history, whose hero belatedly accepts political change, but then dies before he has a chance to redefine himself in regard to that acceptance.

Introduction

William Hazlitt, writing in 1816, gave us what seems to me the most
provocative criticism that Shakespeare's *Coriolanus* has received. Beginning with the observation that the play was "a storehouse of political commonplaces," Hazlitt sadly observed that Shakespeare, unlike himself, seemed a man of the Right, if only because "the cause
of the people is indeed but little calculated as a subject for poetry." It
might be salutary if many of our contemporary students of literature, who wish to make of it an instrument for social change, would
meditate upon Hazlitt's profound reflections on poetry's love of
power:

> The language of poetry naturally falls in with the language
> of power. The imagination is an exaggerating and exclu-
> sive faculty: it takes from one thing to add to another: it
> accumulates circumstances together to give the greatest
> possible effect to a favourite object. The understanding is
> a dividing and measuring faculty, it judges of things not
> according to their immediate impression on the mind, but
> according to their relations to one another. The one is a
> monopolising faculty, which seeks the greatest quantity of
> present excitement by inequality and disproportion; the
> other is a distributive faculty, which seeks the greatest
> quantity of ultimate good, by justice and proportion. The
> one is an aristocratical, the other a republican faculty. The
> principle of poetry is a very anti-levelling principle. It aims
> at effect, it exists by contrast. It admits of no medium. It
> is everything by excess. It rises above the ordinary stan-
> dard of sufferings and crimes. It presents a dazzling ap-

pearance. It shows its head turretted, crowned, and crested. Its front is gilt and blood-stained. Before it "it carries noise, and behind it leaves tears." It has its altars and its victims, sacrifices, human sacrifices. Kings, priests, nobles, are its train-bearers, tyrants and slaves its executioners.—"Carnage is its daughter."—Poetry is right-royal. It puts the individual for the species, the one above the infinite many, might before right. A lion hunting a flock of sheep or a herd of wild asses is a more poetical object than they; and we even take part with the lordly beast, because our vanity or some other feeling makes us disposed to place ourselves in the situation of the strongest party. So we feel some concern for the poor citizens of Rome when they meet together to compare their wants and grievances, till Coriolanus comes in and with blows and big words drives this set of "poor rats," this rascal scum, to their homes and beggary before him. There is nothing heroical in a multitude of miserable rogues not wishing to be starved, or complaining that they are like to be so; but when a single man comes forward to brave their cries and to make them submit to the last indignities, from mere pride and self-will, our admiration of his prowess is immediately converted into contempt for their pusillanimity. The insolence of power is stronger than the plea of necessity. The tame submission to usurped authority or even the natural resistance to it has nothing to excite or flatter the imagination: it is the assumption of a right to insult or oppress others that carries an imposing air of superiority with it. We had rather be the oppressor than the oppressed. The love of power in ourselves and the admiration of it in others are both natural to man: the one makes him a tyrant, the other a slave.

Even I initially resist the dark implications of Hazlitt's crucial insight: "The principle of poetry is a very anti-levelling principle." Wallace Stevens, who like Hazlitt and Nietzsche took the lion as the emblem of poetry, tells us that poetry is a destructive force: "The lion sleeps in the sun . . . / It could kill a man." Hazlitt, an unreconstructed Jacobin, writes with the authority of the strongest literary critic that the European Left has yet produced. I prefer him to T. S.

Eliot on *Coriolanus,* not just because Eliot writes with the grain politically, as it were, and Hazlitt against it, but because the Romantic
critic also understands the drama's family romance better than the
poet of *The Waste Land* does.

Eliot certainly was fonder of Coriolanus than Hazlitt could find
it in himself to be. I cannot quarrel with Hazlitt's account of the
Roman hero's motivations: "Coriolanus complains of the fickleness
of the people: yet, the instant he cannot gratify his pride and obsti-
nacy at their expense, he turns his arms against his country." When
Volumnia cries out for the pestilence to strike all trades and occupations in Rome, because they have defied her son, Hazlitt allows himself a splendidly mordant comment:

> This is but natural: it is but natural for a mother to have
> more regard for her son than for a whole city; but then the
> city should be left to take some care of itself. The care of
> the state cannot, we here see, be safely entrusted to mater-
> nal affection, or to the domestic charities of high life. The
> great have private feelings of their own, to which the in-
> terests of humanity and justice must courtesy. Their inter-
> ests are so far from being the same as those of the com-
> munity, that they are in direct and necessary opposition to
> them; their power is at the expense of *our* weakness; their
> riches of *our* poverty; their pride of *our* degradation; their
> splendour of *our* wretchedness; their tyranny of *our* servi-
> tude. If they had the superior knowledge ascribed to them
> (which they have not) it would only render them so much
> more formidable; and from Gods would convert them into
> Devils. The whole dramatic moral of *Coriolanus* is that
> those who have little shall have less, and that those who
> have much shall take all that others have left. The people
> are poor; therefore they ought to be starved. They are
> slaves; therefore they ought to be beaten. They work hard;
> therefore they ought to be treated like beasts of burden.
> They are ignorant; therefore they ought not to be allowed
> to feel that they want food, or clothing, or rest, that they
> are enslaved, oppressed, and miserable. This is the logic of
> the imagination and the passions; which seek to aggran-
> dize what excites admiration and to heap contempt on
> misery, to raise power into tyranny, and to make tyranny

absolute; to thrust down that which is low still lower, and to make wretches desperate: to exalt magistrates into kings, kings into gods; to degrade subjects to the rank of slaves, and slaves to the condition of brutes. The history of mankind is a romance, a mask, a tragedy, constructed upon the principles of *poetical justice;* it is a noble or royal hunt, in which what is sport to the few is death to the many, and in which the spectators halloo and encourage the strong to set upon the weak, and cry havoc in the chase though they do not share in the spoil. We may depend upon it that what men delight to read in books, they will put in practice in reality.

Poetical justice is not political or social justice, because it ensues from the royal hunt of the imagination. Hazlitt is not concerned that this should be so; poetry and power marry one another. His proper concern, as a literary critic who would die for social change if he could, is that we protect ourselves, not against literature, but against those who would make a wrong because literal use of the poetics of power. Shrewd as Hazlitt's political insight is, his best insight into the play comes when he contrasts the attitudes toward Coriolanus of Volumnia, his mother, and Virgilia, his wife: "The one is only anxious for his honour; the other is fearful for his life." Glory indeed is Volumnia's obsession; Shakespeare makes her Homeric, a sort of female Achilles, while Coriolanus is more like Virgil's Turnus (as Howard Felperin notes), which may be why his wife is named Virgilia. What is most problematical in *Coriolanus* is the hero's relationship to his fierce mother, a relationship unique in Shakespeare.

II

Volumnia hardly bears discussion, once we have seen that she would be at home wearing armor in *The Iliad.* She is about as sympathetic as the Greek heroes in Shakespeare's *Troilus and Cressida.* Coriolanus himself sustains endless analysis and meditation; even the question of our sympathy for him is forever open. Neither a beast nor a god, he is a great soldier, far greater even than Antony or Othello. Indeed, to call him merely a great soldier seems quite inadequate. He is a one-man army, unique and pure, a sport of nurture rather than of nature, a dreadful monument to his mother's remorseless drive, her will-to-power. Perhaps he resembles Spenser's Talus, the iron man, more even than he suggests Virgil's Turnus. He has no military weaknesses, and no civilian strengths. Politically he is a walking and breathing disaster, in a play that persistently imposes politics upon him. The play would fail if Coriolanus were totally unsympathetic to us, and clearly the play is very strong, though its virtues do not make less weird Eliot's celebrated judgment that *Hamlet* was an aesthetic failure, while *Coriolanus* was Shakespeare's best tragedy. Hamlet contains us, while Coriolanus does not even contain himself. As several critics have remarked, he is a kind of baby Mars, and is very nearly empty, a moral void. How can a baby nullity possibly be a tragic hero?

For Frank Kermode, *Coriolanus* is a tragedy of ideas, but Kermode is unable to tell us what the ideas are, and though he calls Coriolanus a great man, he also does not tell us in just what that greatness consists. I may be unjust to Kermode if the crucial idea turns out to be solipsism and if the greatness of Coriolanus is in his imperfect solipsism which cannot become perfect so long as Volumnia is alive. But solipsism, perfect or not, constitutes greatness in a poet, rather than in a tragic hero. Milton's Satan is an almost perfect solipsist, and that, rather than his splendid wickedness, is why he is a heroic villain and not the hero of a cosmic tragedy. Satan is a great poet, almost the archetype of the modern strong poet (as I have written elsewhere). Coriolanus has no imagination and is no poet at all, except when he provokes his own catastrophe.

Kenneth Burke's *Coriolanus* is a tragedy of the grotesque, which I translate as meaning that politics and the grotesque are one and the same, and that seems fair and true enough. Coriolanus is to Burke a master of invective, rather like Shakespeare's Timon, and the wielder of invective makes a convincing tragic scapegoat. That gives us still the question of this hero's eminence; is he more than a great (and prideful) killing machine? A. D. Nuttall, in his admirable study of Shakespearean mimesis, finds the warrior's aristocratic spirit to be both large and shallow, "at one and same time a sort of Titan and a baby." But how can we get at the Titanism, or is it actually a mockery of the old giants, so that Coriolanus is merely a prophecy of General George Patton? Nuttall shrewdly takes away everything he gives Coriolanus, whose "character is one of great pathos," but: "The pathos lies in the fact that he has no inside." Again, Nuttall salutes Coriolanus for one moment of "true Stoic grandeur," when he replies to banishment with: "I banish you." Nuttall then adds that we see a red-faced child in a temper tantrum. As Nuttall says, this is superb mimesis, but can we greatly care what happens to such a hero? In Homer, the answer would be affirmative, since Achilles is at least as much a spoiled child as Coriolanus is. Yet Achilles is a poet also, a powerful imagination brooding bitterly upon its own mortality, and so we care what happens to him. His greatness is convincing not just because others reflect it to us, but because his eloquence is universally persuasive.

Harold C. Goddard, the most generous and perceptive of all Shakespearean critics, finds the one fault of Coriolanus to be that he "lacks unconsciousness of his virtue." Less generously, we could label Coriolanus an instance of "Mars as narcissist," rather than Goddard's "proud idealist" who is entirely a victim of his virago of a mother. Perhaps the ambivalence that Coriolanus provokes in us can be set aside if we contemplate his heroic death scene, wholly appropriate for a tragic protagonist in Shakespeare:

CORIOLANUS: Hear'st thou, Mars?
AUFIDIUS: Name not the god, thou boy of tears!
CORIOLANUS: Ha?
AUFIDIUS: No more.
CORIOLANUS: Measureless liar, thou hast made my heart
    Too great for what contains it. "Boy"? O slave!
    Pardon me, lords, 'tis the first time that ever
    I was forc'd to scold. Your judgments, my grave
        lords,
    Must give this cur the lie; and his own notion—
    Who wears my stripes impress'd upon him, that
    Must bear my beating to his grave—shall join
    To thrust the lie unto him.
1. LORD: Peace both, and hear me speak.
CORIOLANUS: Cut me to pieces, Volsces, men and lads,
    Stain all your edges on me. "Boy," false hound!
    If you have writ your annals true, 'tis there
    That, like an eagle in a dove-cote, I
    [Flutter'd] your Volscians in Corioles.
    Alone I did it. "Boy"!
AUFIDIUS: Why, noble lords,
    Will you be put in mind of his blind fortune,

> Which was your shame, by this unholy braggart,
> 'Fore your own eyes and ears?
> ALL CONSPIRATORS: Let him die for't.
> ALL PEOPLE: Tear him to pieces! Do it presently!—
>   He kill'd my son!—My daughter!—He kill'd my
>   cousin Marcus!—He kill'd my father!
> 2. LORD: Peace ho! no outrage, peace!
>   The man is noble, and his fame folds in
>   This orb o' th' earth. His last offenses to us
>   Shall have judicious hearing. Stand, Aufidius,
>   And trouble not the peace.
> CORIOLANUS: O that I had him,
>   With six Aufidiuses, or more, his tribe,
>   To use my lawful sword!
> AUFIDIUS: Insolent villain!
> ALL CONSPIRATORS: Kill, kill, kill, kill, kill him!
> *Draw the Conspirators, and kills Martius, who falls.*

This is Coriolanus at his worst and at his best, with the extremes not to be disentangled. His triple repetition of "Boy" reflects his fury both at Aufidius's insolence and at his own subservience to his mother, whose boy he now knows he will never cease to be. Yet his vision of himself as an eagle fluttering his enemies' dove-cotes raises his legitimate pride to an ecstasy in which we share, and we are captured by his exultant and accurate "Alone I did it." There is his tragedy, and his grandeur: "Alone I did it." If they have writ their annals true, then he is content to be cut to pieces by them. His death is tragic because it is a *sparagmos,* not Orphic, but not the death of Turnus either. What is torn apart is the last representative of the heroism that fights alone and wins alone, and that can find no place in the world of the commonal and the communal.

The Herculean Hero

Eugene M. Waith

As Coriolanus marches on Rome at the head of a Volscian army, the Roman general, Cominius, describes him thus to his old enemies, the tribunes:

> He is their god. He leads them like a thing
> Made by some other deity than Nature,
> That shapes man better; and they follow him
> Against us brats with no less confidence
> Than boys pursuing summer butterflies
> Or butchers killing flies.
>
> . . . .
>   He will shake
> Your Rome about your ears
>
>   (4.6, 90–94, 98–99)

To which Menenius adds: "As Hercules / Did shake down mellow fruit." In these words Coriolanus is not only presented as a god and compared to Hercules; he is "like a thing / Made by some other deity than Nature." So extraordinary is he that even his troops, inspired by him, feel themselves to be as much superior to the Romans as boys to butterflies or butchers to flies. Like Menaphon's description of Tamburlaine ("Such breadth of shoulders as might mainly bear / Old Atlas' burthen") and Cleopatra's of Antony ("His legs bestrid

From *The Herculean Hero in Marlowe, Chapman, Shakespeare and Dryden.* © 1962 by Eugene M. Waith. Columbia University Press, 1962 the ocean"), this description of Coriolanus is central to Shakespeare's depiction of his hero. His superhuman bearing and his opposition to Rome are the two most important facts about him.

The godlike qualities of Shakespeare's Coriolanus need to be emphasized in an era which has tended to belittle him. He has been treated recently as a delayed adolescent who has never come to maturity, a "splendid oaf [John Palmer]," a mother's boy, a figure so lacking in dignity that he cannot be considered a tragic hero. The catastrophe has been said to awaken amusement seasoned with contempt. In spite of some impressive protests against this denigration, the heroic stature of one of Shakespeare's largest figures remains somewhat obscured.

That he often cuts an unsympathetic figure (especially in the eyes of the twentieth century) is not surprising. His very superiority repels sympathy, while his aristocratic contempt of the plebeians shocks the egalitarian. His pride and anger provide a convenient and conventional basis of disapproval for those who share the tribunes' view that:

> Caius Marcius was
> A worthy officer i' th' war, but insolent,
> O'ercome with pride, ambitious past all thinking,
> Self-loving—
>
> (4.6.29–32)

Pride and anger, as we have seen [elsewhere], are among the distinguishing characteristics of the Herculean hero; without them he would not be what he is.

In one major respect the story of Coriolanus departs from that of his heroic prototype: Coriolanus submits to the entreaties of Volumnia and spares Rome. At this moment he is more human and more humane than at any other in the play, and it is the decision of this moment which leads directly to his destruction. Ironically, the one action of which most of his critics approve is "most mortal" to him. He is murdered not so much because he is proud as because of an intermission in his pride.

The portrait of Coriolanus is built up by means of contrasts. Some of them are absolute, such as those with the people and the tribunes. Others are modified by resemblances: the contrasts with his fellow-patricians, his enemy Aufidius, and his mother Volumnia. Such a dialectical method of presentation is reminiscent of Seneca and recalls even more precisely the technique of Marlowe in *Tambur-laine*. Something closely akin to it is used in *Bussy D'Ambois* and *Antony and Cleopatra*. In all of these plays sharply divergent views of the hero call attention to an essential paradox in his nature. The technique is brilliantly suited to the dramatization of such heroes, but, as the critical response to these plays has shown, it has the disadvantage of stirring serious doubts about the genuineness of the heroism. Readers, as opposed to spectators, have been especially susceptible to these misgivings, since they had before them no actor to counter by the very nobility of his bearing the devastating effect of hostile views. Readers of *Coriolanus* seem to have adopted some or all of the opposition views of the hero's character.

The contrast between Coriolanus and the citizens of Rome is antipodal. Whatever he most basically is they are not, and this contrast is used as the introduction to his character. The "mutinous citizens" who occupy the stage as the play begins are not entirely a despicable lot. It is clear enough that they represent a dangerous threat to the established order, but some of them speak with wisdom and tolerance. For one citizen who opposes Coriolanus because "he's a very dog to the commonalty" (ll. 28–29) there is another who recalls the warrior's services to Rome, and resentment of his pride is balanced against recognition of his lack of covetousness. These citizens, in their opening words and later in their conversation with Menenius, are neither remarkably bright nor stupid, neither models of good nature nor of malice. They are average people, and this may be the most important point about them. Their failings are as common as their virtues: in both we see the limitations of their horizons. Incapable of heroic action themselves, they are equally incapable of understanding a heroic nature. The more tolerant citizen in the first scene excuses the pride of Coriolanus by saying he cannot help it (l. 42), and hence should not be judged too harshly. In a later scene the citizens complain to Coriolanus that he doesn't love them. One of them tells him that the price of the consulship is "to ask it kindly" (2.3.81), a demand which has received enthusiastic approval from several modern critics. The citizens want the great warrior to be jolly and friendly with them, so that they may indulge in the luxury of treating him as a lovable eccentric. From the moment of his first entrance it is obvious that he will never allow them this luxury.

The first impression we are given of him is of his intemperance and his scorn of the people. Menenius Agrippa, one that, in the words of the Second Citizen, "hath always loved the people," has just cajoled them with his fable of the belly into a less rebellious mood when the warrior enters and delivers himself of a blistering tirade. The citizens are "dissentious rogues," "scabs," "curs," "hares," "geese," finally "fragments." He reminds them of their cowardice and inconstancy. But the most devastating part of his speech is the accusation that the citizens prefer to give their allegiance to a man humbled by a punishment which they will call unjust:

> Your virtue is
> To make him worthy whose offense subdues him
> And curse that justice did it.
>
> (1.1.178–80)

What they cannot tolerate except in the crises of war is a greatness which lifts a man far beyond their reach.

In making his accusations Caius Marcius, as he is then called, reveals his reverence for valour, constancy and a great spirit, as well as his utter contempt for those who will never attain such virtues. We may suspect immediately what the rest of the play makes clear, that these are his own virtues. However, since they are displayed by a speech whose tone is so angry and contemptuous—so politically outrageous, when compared to the clever performance of Menenius—they are less apt to win liking than respect. We are confronted by the extraordinary in the midst of the average, a whole man amidst "fragments."

In succeeding scenes with the citizenry the indications of the first scene are developed. The battle at Corioles, where he wins his cognomen Coriolanus, is of course the key scene for the demonstration of valour, "the chiefest virtue," as Cominius later reminds the senators in describing the exploits of Coriolanus (2.2.87–88). Before the sally of the Volscians the Roman soldiers flee in miserable confusion, providing a pat example of their cowardice and bringing on themselves another volley of curses from their leader. Everything in the scene heightens the contrast between him and them. "I'll leave the foe / And make my wars on you!" he threatens; "Follow me!" (1.4.39–42). When his courageous pursuit of the Volscians into their city is followed by the closing of their gate we are presented with the ultimate contrast and an emblem of the hero's situation: he is one against the many, whether the many are enemies or fellow countrymen. As Shakespeare presents this astounding feat it borders on the supernatural. Coriolanus is given Herculean strength. The simple statement of a soldier sums it up: "He is himself alone, / To answer all the city (ll.51–52). Titus Lartius, supposing him dead, adds an encomium in which the qualities he has just demonstrated are converted into an icon:

> A carbuncle entire, as big as thou art,
> Were not so rich a jewel. Thou wast a soldier
> Even to Cato's wish, not fierce and terrible
> Only in strokes, but with thy grim looks and
> The thunder-like percussion of thy sounds
> Thou mad'st thine enemies shake, as if the world
> Were feverous and did tremble.
>
> (1.4.55–61)

When the battle is won, the soldiers set about plundering the city; Caius Marcius, matching his valour with generosity, refuses any reward but the name of Coriolanus which he has earned. No doubt there is a touch of pride in such conspicuous self-denial, but the magnificence of the gesture is what counts. It is not contrasted with true humility but with pusillanimity and covetousness.

Coriolanus is not indifferent to the opinion of others, but he insists upon being valued for his accomplishments, and not for "asking kindly":

> Better it is to die, better to starve,
> Than crave the hire which first we do deserve.
>
> (2.3.120–21)

The question of his absolute worth—the central question of the play—is posed in an uncompromising form in the scenes where Coriolanus is made to seek the approval of the citizens. Though his reluctance to boast of his exploits, to show his wounds, or to speak to the people with any genuine warmth does not immediately lose him their votes, it has cost him the approval of many critics. In itself, however, this reluctance stems from a virtue and a major one. He refuses to seem other than he is and refuses to change his principles to suit the situation. The citizens, meanwhile, unsure what to think, first give him their "voices," and then are easily persuaded by the tribunes to change their minds. Again the contrast is pat, and however unlovely the rigidity of Coriolanus may be, its merit is plain when seen next to such paltry shifting. That it is a terrible and in

some ways inhuman merit is suggested in the ironical words of the
tribune Brutus: "You speak o' th' people / As if you were a god to
punish, not / A man of their infirmity" (3.1.80–82). Later Menenius
says without irony: "His nature is too noble for the world. / He
would not flatter Neptune for his trident / Or Jove for's power to
thunder" (3.1.255–57).

The greatness of Coriolanus is seen not only in his extraordinary valour and generosity but in his absolute rejection of anything
in which he does not believe. In this scene he is urged to beg for
something which he deserves, to flatter people whom he despises,
and to conceal or modify his true beliefs. His refusal to do any of
these things is manifested in a crescendo of wrath, defending his
heroic integrity. The culmination is a violent denunciation of the
plebeians for their ignorance, cowardice, disloyalty and inconsist-
ency. Both friends and enemies attempt to stop the flow of this tirade, but Coriolanus rushes on with the force of an avalanche. The
quality of the speech can be seen only in an extensive quotation:

> No, take more!
> What may be sworn by, both divine and human,
> Seal what I end withal! This double worship—
> Where one part does disdain with cause, the other
> Insult without all reason; where gentry, title, wisdom
> Cannot conclude but by the yea and no
> Of general ignorance—it must omit
> Real necessities, and give way the while
> To unstable slightness. Purpose so barr'd, it follows
> Nothing is done to purpose. Therefore, beseech you—
> You that will be less fearful than discreet;
> That love the fundamental part of state
> More than you doubt the change on't; that prefer
> A noble life before a long, and wish
> To jump a body with a dangerous physic
> That's sure of death without it—at once pluck out
> The multitudinous tongue; let them not lick
> The sweet which is their poison. Your dishonour
> Mangles true judgment, and bereaves the state
> Of that integrity which should become't,
> Not having the power to do the good it would
> For th'ill which doth control't.

(3.1.140–61)

It seems almost impertinent to object to the lack of moderation in this speech. In the great tumble of words, whose forward movement is constantly altered and augmented by parenthetical developments, excess is as characteristic of the presentation as of the emotions expressed, yet one hardly feels that such excess is a matter of degree. What is conveyed here could not be brought within the range of a normally acceptable political statement by modifying here and there an overforceful phrase. It is of another order entirely, and excess is its mode of being. The words of Coriolanus's denunciation of the plebeians are the exact analogue of the sword-strokes with which he fights his way alone into Corioles. Rapid, violent and unbelievably numerous, they express the wrath which accompanies heroic valour. However horrifying they may be, they are also magnificent. Both approval and disapproval give way to awe, as they do in the terrible scenes of Hercules' wrath.

In the scenes which bring to a culmination the quarrel of Coriolanus and the Roman people the great voice of the hero is constantly surrounded by lesser voices which oppose it—the friends, who urge moderation, the tribunes, who foment discord, and the people, who respond to each new suggestion. The words "tongue," "mouth" and "voice" are reiterated, "voice" often having the meaning of "vote." We hear the scorn of Coriolanus for the voices of the many in his words: "The tongues o' th' common mouth," "Have I had children's voices?" "Must these have voices, that can yield them now / And straight disclaim their tongues? . . . You being their mouths, why rule you not their teeth?" "at once pluck out / The multitudinous tongue" (3.1.22, 30, 34–36, 155–56). As for the hero, we are told by Menenius, "His heart's his mouth; / What his breast forges, that his tongue must vent" (3.1.257–58), and when, shortly after, the "multitudinous tongue" accuses him of being a traitor to the people, he makes the speech which leads directly to his banishment: "The fires i' th' lowest hell fold-in the people!" (3.3.68). It is the final answer of the heroic voice to the lesser voices.

The contrast is also realized dramatically in the movement of these scenes, for around the figure of Coriolanus, standing his ground and fighting, the crowd swirls and eddies. Coriolanus and the patricians enter to a flourish of trumpets; to them the tribunes enter. After the hero's lengthy denunciation of the people, they are sent for by the tribunes. The stage business is clearly indicated in the directions: "Enter a rabble of *Plebeians* with the *Aediles*." "*They all bustle about Coriolanus.*" "*Coriolanus draws his sword.*" "*In this mutiny*

the Tribunes, the Aediles, and the People are beat in." "A noise within."
"Enter *Brutus* and *Sicinius* with the *Rabble* again" (3.1.180, 185, 223,
229, 260, 263).

If Shakespeare does not make the many-voiced, ceaselessly
shifting people hateful, he also makes it impossible to respect them.
M. W. MacCallum shows that while the people are given more reason to fear Coriolanus than they are in Plutarch, their original uprising is made considerably less justifiable. Whether or not Shakespeare
reveals a patrician bias in his portrayal of them, there can be no doubt
that he shares the distrust of popular government common to his
time. Condescension qualifies whatever sympathy he shows.

Coriolanus cannot be condescended to. He belongs to another
world, as he makes clear in his final denunciation of the people in
response to their verdict of banishment:

> You common cry of curs, whose breath I hate
> As reek o' th' rotten fens, whose loves I prize
> As the dead carcasses of unburied men
> That do corrupt my air, I banish you!
>
> . . . .
>   Despising
> For you the city, thus I turn my back.
> There is world elsewhere.
>
> (3.3.120–23, 133–35)

That world is the forbidding world of heroes, from which he promises his friends:

> you shall
> Hear from me still, and never of me aught
> But what is like me formerly.
>
> (4.1.51–53)

The tribunes are portrayed much less favourably than the
people, though, surprisingly, they have eager apologists among the
critics. Less foolish than the plebeians, they are more malicious. Motivated by political ambition, they provoke sedition, encouraging the
plebeians to change their votes, and baiting Coriolanus with insults.
When the exiled Coriolanus is marching on Rome "like a thing /
Made by some other deity than nature," they appear almost as small
and insignificant as the people themselves.

The contrast with these scheming politicians establishes the honesty of Coriolanus and his lack of ulterior motives. He has political convictions rather than ambitions. Though he believes that his services to Rome deserve the reward of the consulship, the wielding of political power does not in itself interest him, nor is it necessary to him as an expression of authority. He is dictatorial without being like a modern dictator. The tribunes, who accuse him of pride, are fully as jealous of their prerogatives as he is, and far more interested in increasing them. Coriolanus's nature, compared to theirs, seems both larger and more pure.

Certain aspects of this heroic nature come out most clearly in contrasts between Coriolanus and his fellow patricians. Menenius is to Coriolanus what Horatio is to Hamlet. Horatio's poise and his freedom from the tyranny of passion show him to be what would be called today a "better adjusted" person than Hamlet; yet Hamlet's lack of what he admires in his friend reveals the stresses of a much rarer nature. No one mistakes Horatio for a hero. Similarly, Menenius is far better than Coriolanus at "getting on" with people. In the first scene of the play his famous fable of the belly, told with a fine combination of good humour and firmness, calms the plebeians. When Coriolanus, after his glorious victory, objects to soliciting votes by showing his wounds in the Forum, Menenius urges, "Pray you go fit you to the custom" (2.2.146). After the banishment he says to the tribunes in a conciliating fashion, "All's well, and might have been much better if / He could have temporiz'd" (4.6.16–17). Menenius's ability to temporize and fit himself to the custom has made him liked on all sides, but this striking evidence of political success does not guarantee him the unqualified respect of the spectator. Dennis erred only in exaggerating, when he called Menenius a buffoon.

In contrast to this jolly patrician, always ready to compromise, the austerity and fixity of Coriolanus stand out. To Plutarch, writing as a moralist and historian, it is lamentable that Coriolanus lacks "the gravity and affability that is gotten with judgement of learning and reason, which only is to be looked for in a governor of state," but though the lack is equally apparent in Shakespeare's tragedy, the conclusion to be drawn differs as the point of view of tragedy differs from that of history. Plutarch judges Coriolanus as a potential governor. He finds that a deficient education has made him "too full of passion and choler" and of wilfulness, which Plutarch says "is the thing of the world, which a governor of a commonwealth for pleasing should shun, being that which Plato called solitariness." The tragedy of *Coriolanus,* for all its political concern, is not contrived to expose either the deficiencies of the protagonist as a governor (though all the evidence is presented) or the unreliability of the plebeians and their representatives (which could be taken for granted). What Shakespeare insists on is an extraordinary force of will and a terrible "solitariness" characteristic of this hero. No contrast in the play brings these out more clearly than the contrast with Menenius.

The change in emphasis from history to the heroic is clearly evident in Shakespeare's treatment of Aufidius. In Plutarch's account he is not mentioned until the time of the banishment, when Coriolanus offers himself as a general to the Volsces. At this point, however, Plutarch states that Aufidius was noble and valiant, that the two had often encountered in battle and that they had "a marvellous private hate one against the other." From these hints Shakespeare makes the figure of the worthy antagonist, who is a part of the story of so many heroes. The rivalry is mentioned in the very first scene of the play, and is made one of the deepest motives of the hero's conduct. He envies the nobility of Aufidius,

> And were I anything but what I am,
> I would wish me only he. . . .
> Were half to half the world by th'ears, and he
> Upon my party, I'd revolt, to make
> Only my wars with him. He is a lion
> That I am proud to hunt.
>
> (1.1.235–40)

To fight with Aufidius is the ultimate test of Coriolanus's valour—of his warrior's areté. And because the rival warrior most nearly shares his own ideals, the relationship takes on an intense intimacy. Shakespeare introduces Aufidius unhistorically into the battle at Corioles. We discover that although Aufidius reciprocates the feelings of Coriolanus, he is prepared after his defeat at Corioles to use dishonourable means, if necessary, to destroy his enemy, but of this Coriolanus knows nothing, nor is there any hint of it when Aufidius later welcomes Coriolanus as an ally:

> Let me twine
> Mine arms about that body whereagainst
> My grained ash an hundred times hath broke

And scarr'd the moon with splinters.

. . . .
                    Know thou first,
I lov'd the maid I married; never man
Sigh'd truer breath. But that I see thee here,
Thou noble thing, more dances my rapt heart
Than when I first my wedded mistress saw
Bestride my threshold.

                            (4.5.111–14, 118–23)

Plutarch's Aufidius makes only a brief and formal speech acknowledging the honour Coriolanus does him. Shakespeare's invention of
a long speech, loaded with the metaphors of love, is the more striking at this point, since the preceding speech by Coriolanus follows
Plutarch very closely indeed. The strong bond between the rival
warriors is obviously important.

It is sometimes thought highly ironic that Coriolanus, who
prides himself on his constancy, should be guilty of the supreme
inconstancy of treason to his country. In fact, however reprehensible
he may be, he is not inconstant. Shakespeare makes it clear that his
first allegiance is always to his personal honour. The fickleness of the
mob and the scheming of the tribunes have deprived him of his de-
serts, much as Agamemnon's seizure of Briseis deprives Achilles.
Both this threat to his honour and an ambivalent love-hatred draw
Coriolanus to the enemy whom he considers almost an alter ego.

Resemblances or fancied resemblances between the two warriors establish the supremacy of the heroic ideal in Coriolanus's scale
of values, but we cannot doubt which of them more nearly encom-
passes the ideal. As we watch the progress of their alliance, we see
Aufidius becoming increasingly jealous and finally working for the
destruction of his rival even while he treats him almost as a mistress.
In defence of his conduct he asserts that Coriolanus has seduced his
friends with flattery, but there is no evidence to support this unlikely
accusation. Malice and double-dealing are quite absent from the nature of Coriolanus.

The ill-will mixed with Aufidius's love serves another purpose
than contrast, however: it adds considerable weight to his praise of
Coriolanus to other characters, such as that contained in a long
speech to his lieutenant:

All places yield to him ere he sits down,
And the nobility of Rome are his;

The senators and patricians love him too.
The tribunes are no soldiers, and their people
Will be as rash in the repeal as hasty
To expel him thence. I think he'll be to Rome
As is the osprey to the fish, who takes it
By sovereignty of nature. First he was
A noble servant to them, but he could not
Carry his honours even. Whether 'twas pride,
Which out of daily fortune ever taints
The happy man; whether defect of judgment,
To fail in the disposing of those chances
Which he was lord of; or whether nature,
Not to be other than one thing, not moving
From th' casque to th' cushion, but commanding peace
Even with the same austerity and garb
As he controll'd the war; but one of these
(As he hath spices of them all, not all,
For I dare so far free him) made him fear'd,
So hated, and so banish'd. But he has a merit
To choke it in the utt'rance. So our virtues
Lie in th' interpretation of the time;
And power, unto itself most commendable,
Hath not a tomb so evident as a chair
T'extol what it hath done.
One fire drives out one fire; one nail, one nail;
Rights by rights falter, strengths by strengths do fail.
Come, let's away. When, Caius, Rome is thine,
Thou art poor'st of all; then shortly art thou mine.

(4.7.28–57)

Surely, what is most remarkable in this account of failure is the
emphasis on virtue. One thinks of Monsieur, telling Guise that Nature's gift of virtue is responsible for the death to which Bussy has-
tens at that very moment, led on by plots of Monsieur's contriving.
In both cases the interests of the speaker are so exactly contrary to
the tenor of their remarks that the character-analysis is given the
force of absolute truth. Aufidius's speech has to be taken in its en-
tirety, so dependent are its component parts on one another. Its
frame is a realistic appraisal of the situation at Rome and of his own
malicious purposes. Within is an intricate structure of praise and

underlies the entire speech: the superiority of Coriolanus to Rome is as much in the order of nature as is the predominance of the osprey, who was thought to have the power of fascinating fish. Next comes Coriolanus's lack of equilibrium, a point which the play has thoroughly established. Aufidius then mentions three possible causes of failure, carefully qualifying the list by saying that in all probability only one was operative. Pride, the first, is presented as the natural temptation of the happy man, as it is in the medieval conception of fortune's wheel. The defect of judgment, mentioned next, recalls the contrast with Menenius, and the patent inability of Coriolanus to take advantage of his situation—to dispose "of those chances / Which he was lord of." Thus, the first cause of failure is a generic fault of the fortunate, while the second is a fault which distinguishes Coriolanus from a lesser man. The third is the inflexibility which makes him austere and fierce at all times. This is not only the most persuasive as an explanation of his troubles but is also the most characteristic of him. The comments which follow immediately—on the "merit to choke it in the utt'rance" and the virtues which "lie in th' interpretation of the time"—suggest redeeming features. They are not simply good qualities which can be balanced against the bad, but virtues inherent in some of the faults which have just been enumerated, or qualities which might be interpreted as either virtues or faults. The inflexibility is the best example. It is closely related to the other faults, to the lack of equilibrium, the pride, and the defect of judgment. Yet it is impossible to regard Coriolanus's refusal to compromise as entirely a fault. It is also his greatest strength. The concluding lines of the speech put forth a paradox even more bewildering, that power, rights and strengths often destroy themselves. Aufidius need only wait for his rival's success to have him in his power. The final emphasis falls entirely on virtue, with no mention of weakness or deficiency.

The eloquent couplet which sums up this paradox,

> One fire drives out one fire; one nail, one nail;
> Rights by rights falter, strengths by strengths do fail

is very like the lines . . . from Chapman's nearly contemporaneous *Tragedy of Charles, Duke of Byron:*

> We have not any strength but weakens us,
> No greatness but doth crush us into air.
> Our knowledges do light us but to err.

From this melancholy point of view the hero is only more certainly doomed than the average man.

Next to Coriolanus Volumnia is the most interesting character in the play—the Roman mother, whose influence over her son is so great and ultimately so fatal. In the first scene a citizen says of Coriolanus's services to Rome, "Though soft-conscienc'd men can be content to say it was for his country, he did it to please his mother and to be partly proud, which he is, even to the altitude of his virtue" (ll. 37–41). In the last act Coriolanus says,

> O my mother, mother! O!
> You have won a happy victory to Rome;
> But for your son—believe it, O believe it!—
> Most dangerously you have with him prevail'd,
> If not most mortal to him.
>
> (5.3.185–89)

But powerful and obvious as this influence is, it should not be allowed to obscure the major differences between mother and son. Volumnia belongs to the world which Coriolanus, as hero, both opposes and seeks to redeem. She represents the city of Rome much more completely than Zenocrate represents the city of Damascus. She is by far the strongest of the forces which Rome brings to bear on him, and much of her strength derives from the fact that she seems at first so thoroughly committed to everything in which he believes. Only gradually do we discover what she truly represents.

In her first scene she is every inch the mother of a warrior, shocking timid Virgilia with grim speeches about a soldier's honour. We next see her welcome Coriolanus after his victory at Corioles, and make the significant remark that only one thing is wanting to fulfil her dreams—one thing "which I doubt not but / Our Rome will cast upon thee" (2.1.217–18)—obviously the consulship. Her son's reply foreshadows the conflict between them:

> Know, good mother,
> I had rather be their servant in my way
> Than sway with them in theirs.
>
> (2.1.218–20)

Volumnia wants power for her son as much as Lady Macbeth wants it for her husband. Coriolanus wants above all to do things "in his way."

Close to the center of the play occurs the first of the two conflicts between mother and son. There is no basis for the scene in Plutarch. It is an addition of great importance, contributing to the characterization of the principals and preparing for the famous interview in which Coriolanus is deterred from his vengeance on Rome. The issues engaged here are what separate Coriolanus from every other character.

He has just delivered his lengthy excoriation of the people, and is being urged by his friends to apologize. As Volumnia enters he asks her if she would wish him to be milder—to be false to his nature, and she, who proclaimed to Virgilia that life was not too great a price to pay for honour, gives him an answer based solely on political expediency: "I would have had you put your power well on, / Before you had worn it out" (3.2.17–18). She observes with great shrewdness, "You might have been enough the man you are / With striving less to be so," but she adds a sentence which shows that what she is advocating is politic concealment of Coriolanus's true nature:

> Lesser had been
> The thwarting of your dispositions, if
> You had not show'd them how ye were dispos'd
> Ere they lack'd power to cross you.
> (ll. 19–23)

In the previous scene, where Coriolanus defied the people and the tribunes, the sincerity of his voice as compared to theirs was expressed in Menenius's words, "His heart's his mouth; / What his breast forges, that his tongue must vent." The same imagery is caught up here in the words in which Volumnia characterizes her attitude towards apologizing:

> I have a heart as little apt as yours,
> But yet a brain that leads my use of anger
> To better vantage.
> (ll. 29–31)

It is not in the least surprising that Menenius applauds this speech, as he does a later and longer one in which Volumnia urges Coriolanus to speak to the people not what his heart prompts,

> But with such words that are but roted in
> Your tongue, though but bastards and syllables

nature. Tamburlaine is obliged to accept the limitations of nature only when he is faced with death; the situation forces Coriolanus to submit sooner. As Hermann Heuer says, " 'Nature' becomes the key-word of the great scene" of the hero's second conflict with his formidable mother. As he sees them approach, the battle is already engaged in his mind between nature and heroic constancy:

> Shall I be tempted to infringe my vow
> In the same time 'tis made? I will not.
>
> (5.3.20–21)

And a moment later:

> But out, affection!
> All bond and privilege of nature, break!
> Let it be virtuous to be obstinate.
>
> (ll. 24–26)

> I'll never
> Be such a gosling to obey instinct, but stand
> As if a man were author of himself
> And knew no other kin.
>
> (ll. 34–36)

Nowhere in the play is the conflict between the heroic and the human more clear-cut. Only the demigod which Coriolanus aspires to be could resist the appeal made by Volumnia and Virgilia. Tamburlaine could refuse Zenocrate before the gates of Damascus, but Marlowe made him more nearly the embodiment of a myth. Coriolanus belongs to a more familiar world and his tragedy can be put very generally as the impossibility in this world, as in the world of Bussy D'Ambois, of reliving a myth. Heroic aspiration is not proof here against the urgent reality of human feelings. Already sensing his weakness, Coriolanus begs Virgilia not to urge forgiveness of the Romans, and to Volumnia he says:

> Do not bid me
> Dismiss my soldiers or capitulate
> Again with Rome's mechanics. Tell me not
> Wherein I seem unnatural. Desire not
> T'allay my rages and revenges with
> Your colder reasons.
>
> (ll. 81–86)

There is unconscious irony in the phrase, "colder reasons," for Volumnia's appeal is nothing if not emotional. It begins and ends with the pitiable plight of Coriolanus's family—a direct assault upon his feelings and instincts. Enclosed in this context is the appeal to his honour. No longer does Volumnia urge mixing honour with policy. It is her strategy now to make the course she recommends appear to be dictated by pure honour. She suggests that if he makes peace between the two sides, even the Volscians will respect him (presumably overlooking his abandonment of their cause), while if he goes on to conquer Rome he will wipe out the nobility of his name. Honour as she now presents it is a godlike sparing of offenders:

> Think'st thou it honourable for a noble man
> Still to remember wrongs?
>
> (ll. 154–55)

The final, and successful, appeal, however, is personal:

> This fellow had a Volscian to his mother;
> His wife is in Corioles, and this child
> Like him by chance.
>
> (ll. 178–80)

Aufidius, shortly after, shows that he has understood perfectly the essential nature of the appeal:

> I am glad thou hast set thy mercy and thy honour
> At difference in thee. Out of that I'll work
> Myself a former fortune.
>
> (ll. 200–202)

I have emphasized Volumnia's rhetorical strategy more than the validity of her arguments, because it is important that Coriolanus is broken by a splendid oration. Eloquence, as is well known, was highly prized by the Elizabethans, and we have seen it in Tamburlaine as a further evidence of heroic superiority. But the rhetorical training of the Elizabethans made them acutely aware of the trickiness of oratory, and eloquence on their stage could be a danger-signal as well as a badge of virtue. The case of Volumnia's appeal to Coriolanus is as far from being clear-cut as it could be. The plea for mercy and the forgetting of injuries commands assent; yet one is well aware that the nature of the injuries, and hence the validity of the vow Coriolanus has taken, are never mentioned. If the matter were to be discussed in the manner of the debate in the Trojan council in *Troilus and Cressida,* it would be a question of whether true honour lay in revenging or forgiving an undoubted injury, and whether the hero's loyalty at this point should be to the city which exiled him or to the city whose forces he now leads. As it is, Volumnia's rhetoric identifies the cause of mercy with the lives of the pleaders, and Coriolanus must choose between his vow and his family. He must indeed defy nature if he resists his mother's plea. Of this she is very well aware, and she plays on her son's attachment to her just as she had done previously, when urging on him a course of moderate hypocrisy. After her victory, judgment between the conflicting issues remains as puzzling as it was before.

When Volumnia's lack of principle and her association with the political world of Rome are fully perceived, it becomes more difficult to be sure of the significance of Coriolanus's capitulation. We know from him that it is likely to be "most mortal," and we know that Aufidius will do whatever he can to make it so. We know, that is, that the hero is now a broken man, but has he been ennobled by choosing the course glorified by Volumnia's eloquence? This is not the impression made by the last scenes. MacCallum says, "Still this collapse of Coriolanus's purpose means nothing more than the victory of his strongest impulse. There is no acknowledgement of offence, there is no renovation of character." His choice is a recognition of the claims of nature, but this recognition makes possible no new affirmation such as Antony's after the bitterness of his defeat. Nature, as amoral as fecund, seems to melt the valour and stoic integrity of Antony, but in the new growth stimulated by this nature, valour and integrity appear again, transformed. To Coriolanus nature comes in the guise of a moral duty, which is also a temptation to betray his principles. The idea of fecundity is present only as Volumnia uses it for a persuasive weapon, threatening him with the horror of treading on his mother's womb. The melting that follows this persuasion leads to mere destruction. Nature, instead of opening a new way to the hero, blocks an old one and teaches him his mortal finitude.

The decision Coriolanus is asked to make is an impossible one. In the situation as Shakespeare presents it, it is almost inconceivable that he should deny the claims made by Volumnia; yet in acknowledging them he accomplishes nothing positively good. He avoids an act of shocking inhumanity and thereby surrenders control of his world to the forces of policy and compromise—the enemies of the "noble heart." Volumnia and Virgilia are hailed by the Romans, whose one thought is gratefulness to be alive. In Corioles Aufidius contrives the assassination of the hero, who is of no further use. What Coriolanus says of the scene of his submission might be applied to the entire ending of the play:

> Behold, the heavens do ope,
> The gods look down, and this unnatural scene
> They laugh at.
>
> (5.3.183–85)

For if the natural order seems to be preserved when Coriolanus decides to spare his country, it is wrecked when the one man of principle is defeated and then murdered. The colossal folly of destroying what far outweighs everything that is preserved is sufficient to provoke the laughter of the gods.

Yet the play does not end on the note of ironic laughter. The final note is affirmation. There is no new vision to affirm and no transcendent world to which the hero willingly goes. Coriolanus will not "join flames with Hercules." What the last scene of the play affirms with compelling force is the value of what the world is losing in the death of the hero. The incident of the assassination dramatizes the essential heroism which Coriolanus has displayed throughout the action. Instead of the comfort of an apotheosis we are given the tragic fact of irremediable loss. After the success of the conspiracy even Aufidius is "struck with sorrow," and closes the play with the prophecy: "Yet he shall have a noble memory."

The handling of the assassination scene restores a much needed clarity after the puzzling ambiguities of Coriolanus's submission to his mother. Envy, meanness, and an underhand way of seeking revenge all make Aufidius the equivalent of the tribunes in earlier scenes. He baits Coriolanus in a similar way and provokes an exactly comparable self-assertion on the part of the hero. As the accusation "traitor" inflamed him before, it does so again, but here there is an interesting difference. After calling him traitor, Aufidius addresses him as Marcius, stripping him of his title of Coriolanus, and finally calls him "thou boy of tears" (5.6.84–99), referring of course to his giving in to his mother's plea. Coriolanus protests each term, but it is "boy" which raises him to the height of his rage:

> Boy! O slave!
>
> . . . .

> Cut me to pieces, Volsces. Men and lads,
> Stain all your edges on me. Boy? False hound!
> If you have writ your annals true, 'tis there,
> That, like an eagle in a dovecote, I
> Flutter'd your Volscians in Corioles.
> Alone I did it. Boy?
>
> (5.6.103, 111–16)

What hurts most is the impugning of his manhood—his heroic *virtus*. He asserts it by the magnificently foolhardy reminiscence of his singlehanded victory over the very people he is addressing—"Alone I did it." His words recall the earlier description of him, "He is himself alone, / To answer all the city" (1.4.51–52). Shakespeare's alteration of history, making Coriolanus "alone" is one of the touches which reveals most unequivocally his heroic conception of the character. In Coriolanus the opposition of the individual might of the hero to the superior forces of nature and fate is pushed to the uttermost.

It is characteristic of Shakespeare's Coriolanus that he resents "boy" more than "traitor," for it is clear throughout that the honour and integrity to which Coriolanus is committed are intensely personal. In this respect he resembles Antony in his final moments. When James Thomson wrote his *Coriolanus* in the middle of the eighteenth century, he reversed the order of the accusations. Thomson's Tullus does not call Coriolanus "boy," but he reminds him of his capitulation and condescendingly offers to protect him from the Volscians. Coriolanus, in return, recalls his victory at Corioles, though he says nothing of being alone. Tullus then insults the Romans and finally accuses Coriolanus of being a traitor both to them and to the Volscians. To the slurs on Rome Coriolanus replies:

> Whate'er her blots, whate'er her giddy factions,
> There is more virtue in one single year
> Of *Roman* story, than your *Volscian* annals
> Can boast thro' all your creeping dark duration!

This patriotic emphasis, which Thomson presumably felt necessary as a means of getting sympathy for his hero, makes all the plainer the consequences of Shakespeare's climactic emphasis on Coriolanus as an individual who can never be completely assimilated into a city, his own or another.

John Philip Kemble's acting version combined Thomson and Shakespeare. He kept the patriotic defence of Rome from Thomson, but followed it with the speeches from Shakespeare prompted by the accusation "traitor." The culmination of the interchange is once more the hero's indignant repetition of "boy!," which Kemble made memorable by his way of saying it. Slightly later, Macready was especially pleased that he could rival Kemble's success in the inflection of this crucial monosyllable. These actors, who made "boy!" the high point of their portrayal of heroic dignity, were much closer to the core of Shakespeare's character than are the critics who see him as in fact boyish and small. The whole effect of the last scene depends on a recognition very similar to Cleopatra's after the death of Antony:

> The soldier's pole is fall'n! Young boys and girls
> Are level now with men. The odds is gone,
> And there is nothing left remarkable
> Beneath the visiting moon.
>
> (4.15.65–68)

Coriolanus is angular, granitic, and hence unlovable. Antony's faults are much more easily forgiven than this obduracy. Yet of the two it is Coriolanus who more certainly commands respect and veneration.

Coriolanus—and the Delights of Faction

Kenneth Burke

This [essay] is to involve one of my experiments with the safest and surest kind of prophecy; namely: prophecy after the event. Our job will be to ask how Shakespeare's grotesque tragedy, *Coriolanus,* "ought to be." And we can check on the correctness of our prophecies by consulting the text.

We begin with these assumptions: Since the work is a tragedy, it will require some kind of symbolic action in which some notable form of victimage is imitated, for the purgation, or edification of an audience. The character that is to be sacrificed must be fit for his role as victim; and everything must so fit together that the audience will find the sacrifice plausible and acceptable (thereby furtively participating in the judgment against the victim, and thus even willing the victimage). The expectations and desires of the audience will be shaped by conditions within the play. But the topics exploited for persuasive purposes *within* the play will also have strategic relevance to kinds of "values" and "tensions" that prevail *outside* the play.

There is a benign perversity operating here. In one sense, the aesthetic and the ethical coincide, since a way of life gives rise to a moral code, and the dramatist can exploit this moral code for poetic effects by building up characters that variously exemplify the system of vices and virtues to which the code explicitly or implicitly subscribes. But in another sense the aesthetic and the ethical are at odds,

From *Language as Symbolic Action: Essays on Life, Literature, and Method.* © 1986 by the Regents of the University of California. University of California Press, 1986.

since the dramatist can transform our moral problems into sources of poetic entertainment. Any ethical "thou shalt not" sets up the conditions for an author to engage an audience by depicting characters that variously violate or threaten to violate the "thou shalt not." And many motivational conflicts that might distress us in real life can be transformed into kinds of poetic imitation that engross us. Thus in the realm of the aesthetic we may be delighted by accounts of distress and corruption that would make the moralist quite miserable.

The moral problem, or social tension, that is here to be exploited for the production of the "tragic pleasure" is purely and simply a kind of discord intrinsic to the distinction between upper classes and lower classes. However, a certain "distance" could be got in Shakespeare's day by treating the problem in terms not of contemporary London but of ancient Rome. A somewhat analogous situation is to be seen in Euripides' tragedy of *The Trojan Women,* which appeared some months after the Athenians had destroyed the little island of Melos, though on its face the play was concerned with the Trojan war, the theme of *The Iliad.* When *Coriolanus* appeared there had been considerable rioting due to the Enclosure Acts by which many tenants had been dispossessed of their traditional rights to the land, and were suffering great hardships. Both of these plays may, in their way, have gained strictly contemporary relevance from the allusive exploiting of a "timely topic." But in any case, each was dealing with a distress of much longer duration, in Euripides' case the horrors of war, and in Shakespeare's case the *malaise* of the conflict between the privileged and the underprivileged, as stated in terms of a struggle between the patricians and plebeians of old Rome.

If we are going to "dramatize" such a tension, we shall want first of all a kind of character who in some way helps *intensify* the tension. Where there are any marked differences in social status, in the situation itself there is a kind of "built-in pride," no matter how carefully one might try to mitigate such contrasts. And despite polite attempts to gloss things over, the unresolved situation is intrinsically there. By the nature of the case, it involves *exclusions.*

But for our purposes the main consideration is this: Whereas a hostess, or a diplomat, or an ingratiating politician, or a public relations counsel might go as far as possible towards *toning down* such situations, the dramatist must work his cures by a quite different method. He must find ways to *play them up.* In some respects, therefore, this play will require a kind of character who is designed to help aggravate the uneasiness of the relationship between nobles and commoners.

For this aspect of his role, our chosen victim is obviously a perfect fit. In contrast with the suave Menenius, who has been addressing the mutinous citizens with such a cautious mixture of gravity and humor, our chosen victim's first words to the people are: "What's the matter, you dissentious rogues, / That, rubbing the poor itch of your opinion, / Make yourselves scabs?" Thereafter, again and again, his gruff (or if you will, arrogant) manner of speaking is designed to point up (for the audience) the conflict intrinsic to the class distinctions with which the play is "drastically" concerned. (It's well to recall here that, in earlier medical usage, a "drastic" was the name for the strongest kind of "cathartic." Also, the word derives etymologically from the same root as "drama.")

The Greek word *hubris* sometimes translates best as "pride," sometimes as "excess." And in Athenian law *hubris* was also used to designate a civil offense, an insulting air of superiority, deemed punishable by death. When you note how neatly all three meanings come together in the role of Coriolanus, I think you will realize at least one reason why I find the play so fascinating. The grotesque hero is *excessively* downright, forthright, outright (and even, after his fashion upright), in his unquestioned assumption that the common people are intrinsically inferior to the nobility. Indeed, though the word "noble" suggests to most of us *either* moral *or* social connotations, Coriolanus takes it for granted that only the *socially* noble can have nobility of any sort. (The word appears about seventy-six times in the play. In half of these contexts it is applied to Coriolanus himself. And, to my knowledge, it is never used ironically, as with Mark Antony's transformations of the word "honourable.") Coriolanus is excessive in ways that prepare the audience to relinquish him for his role as scapegoat, in accentuating a trait that the audience also shares with him, though seldom so avowedly.

More "prophesying after the event" is still to be done. But first, perhaps we should pause to give a generalized outline of the plot, having in mind the kind of tension (or factional malaise) that the drama would transform into terms of purgative appeal:

After having gained popular acclaim through prowess in war, a courageous but arrogant patrician, who had been left fatherless when young and was raised by his mother, is persuaded by his mother to sue for high political office. In campaigning, he alienates the plebeians who, goaded by his political rivals, condemn him to exile. When in exile, making an alliance with the commander of the armies he had conquered, he leads a force against his own country. But before the decisive battle, during a visit by his closest relatives, his mother persuades him not to attack. In so doing, she unintentionally sets in motion the conditions whereby the allied commander, whom he had formerly vanquished and who envies his fame, successfully plots his assassination.

It is impressive how perfectly the chosen victim's virtues and vices work together, in fitting him for his sacrificial function. The several scenes in the first act that build up his prowess as a soldier not only endow him with a sufficient measure of the heroics necessary for tragic dignification. They also serve to make it clear why, when he returns to Rome and, against his will, consents to seek the office of consul, he is bound to be a misfit. Shakespeare himself usually gives us the formula for such matters. It is stated by the Tribune, Brutus, in act 3, scene 3: Get him angry, for

> He hath been us'd
> Ever to conquer, and to have his worth
> Of contradiction. Being once chaf'd, he cannot
> Be rein'd again to temperance; then he speaks
> What's in his heart, and that is there which looks
> With us to break his neck.

He is not the "war games" kind of military man, not the "computer mentality"; thus we spontaneously accept it that his valiant though somewhat swashbuckling ways as a warrior will make him incompetent in the wiles of peaceful persuasion, which the wily Shakespeare so persuasively puts in a bad light, *within* the conditions of the play, by his treatment of the Tribunes. Though Shakespeare's theater is, from start to finish, a masterful enterprise in the arts of persuasion, high among his resources is the building of characters who are weak in such devices. Indeed, considered from this point of view, Coriolanus's bluntness is in the same class with Cordelia's fatal inability to flatter Lear. Later we shall find other reasons to think of

Lear in connection with Coriolanus's railings. Meanwhile, note how the Tribunes' skill at petition is portrayed as not much better than mere cunning, even though somewhat justified by our highborn goat's arrogance in his dealings with the commoners. He finds it impossible even to simulate an attitude of deference. And once we have his number, when he sets out to supplicate, armed with the slogan "The word is 'mildly,'" the resources of dramatic irony have already prepared us for the furious outbursts that will get the impetuous war-hero banished from Rome, a climax capped perfectly by his quick rejoinder, "I banish you!" As a fearless fighter, he is trained to give commands and to risk his life, not to supplicate. And the better to build him up, in the role of the Tribunes Shakespeare makes the art of political supplication seem quite unsavory.

All told, Coriolanus's courage and outspokenness make him a sufficiently "noble" character to dignify a play by the sacrificing of him. And excessive ways of constantly reaffirming his assumption that only the *social* nobility can be *morally* noble indicts him for sacrifice. But more than this is needed to make him effectively yieldable.

For one thing, always in drama we encounter a variation on the theme of what I would call the "paradox of substance." A character cannot "be himself" unless many others among the dramatis personae contribute to this end, so that the very essence of a character's nature is in a large measure defined, or determined, by the other characters who variously assist or oppose him. The most obvious instance of what I mean is the role of Aufidius. If it is an integral part of Coriolanus's role to be slain, there must be a slayer. And in this sense Aufidius is "derived from" the character of Coriolanus. The conditions of the play set up Coriolanus as a gerundive, a "to be killed," and Aufidius is to be the primary instrument in the killing. As is typical of a Shakespearean play, just before the close of the first act Aufidius points the arrows of the audience's expectations by announcing to a soldier (and thus to the audience) that he will destroy Coriolanus in whatever way possible. Even so, it's always good if a man speaks with high respect of a slain rival; accordingly, though Aufidius must be plotter enough to fulfill his role in Coriolanus's death, he must be of sufficient dignity so that his final tribute to the "noble memory" of Coriolanus will serve to give the audience a parting reassurance that they have participated in the symbolic sacrifice of a victim worth the killing. The assurance was made doubly necessary by the fact that, just before the slaying, there had been a kind of last-moment revelation, when Aufidius called the bold warrior a "boy of tears," thus propounding a final formula for Coriolanus's relationship to his mother. Aufidius's claims as a worthy opponent (despite his unsavory traits) are established in Coriolanus's first references to him, such as, "I sin in envying his nobility," and "He is a lion / That I am proud to hunt."

This relationship we should dwell on. For it best illustrates just what we mean by "prophesying after the event" in order to "derive" the play in terms of poetics. If the characters are viewed simply as "people," we should treat the relationship between Coriolanus and Volumnia much as Plutarch did, in the "Life" from which Shakespeare borrowed so much of his plot. Coriolanus would thus be interpreted as the offspring of a bellicose, overbearing mother, who sought to compensate for the death of his father by being both mother and father to him. There is one change worth noting. Whereas Plutarch attributes Coriolanus's resultant irritability to womanishness, Shakespeare seems to have settled for a mere failure to outgrow boyishness. But our main point is this: Along the lines of poetic principles, the derivation should be reversed; and instead of viewing Coriolanus as an offspring of his mother, we view her role as a function contributory to his.

Thus, in an early scene, she is portrayed as a pugnacious virago of whom the son became a responsive masculine copy. This portrait of her prepares us to accept it as "natural" that, when he returns from the battlefields, *she* can persuade him, against his wishes, to stand for consul. And thus, later in the play, we will accept it that *she* can persuade him not to attack Rome—and (quite unintentionally on her part) this decision sets up the conditions responsible for his death. In brief, when using her to account for Coriolanus's character in the first place, Shakespeare is preparing her to serve as plausible explanation for two crucial moments in the *plot:* a nonpolitical man's ventures into politics, and a fighting man's failure to join in battle when success was certain. In brief, her relation to Coriolanus motivates for us two decisions of his that are basically necessary, to make the *turns* in the tragedy seem plausible.

I say "turns," having in mind the Aristotelian word, "peripety," to name the striking moment, near the center of a complex plot, when some significant reversal takes place. But I might here pause to note that this is a play of many such reversals. In act 1, there are the many scenes that might in general be entitled the "Tides of Battle," including the one where Coriolanus—or at that time, Caius Marcius, since he has not yet received his new name from the city he conquered—is thought to be lost, through having single-handedly pursued the enemy within the gate of Corioli, fighting alone where Plutarch less theatrically had reported him as but leader of a small band. At the end of act 2, the commoners are persuaded by the Tribunes to retract their intention of voting for Coriolanus as consul. The big peripety is, as one might expect, in act 3, the hero's fatal bursts of rage having been prepared for ironically by his decision to be mild. In this act, there is a kind of peripety-atop-peripety, when Coriolanus retorts to his banishers, "I banish you!"

In act 4, scene 5, there is a neat turn when Aufidius's serving-men, who would treat Coriolanus shabbily when he first appears, abruptly change their tune after he has talked with Aufidius, and the compact against Rome has been agreed on. Besides being one of the few comic spots in the play, this scene is also useful in preparing for the last fatal reversal, since it brings out the fact that, even if Coriolanus and Aufidius are to become allies, Coriolanus's reputation is a threat to Aufidius. Another reversal, in scene 6, occurs when, just after the Tribunes and citizens have been congratulating themselves on the conditions of peace resulting from Coriolanus's banishment, they are startled by the news that Coriolanus is marching on Rome.

In act 5, there is a fatal peripety, when Coriolanus is persuaded by his mother to give up his intention of attacking Rome. This leads to another peripety, the ironic twist whereby, soon after Menenius has explained to one of the Tribunes that Coriolanus will never yield ("There is no more mercy in him than there is milk in a male tiger"), they learn that Coriolanus has begun to withdraw. And even though the arrows of our expectations were clearly pointing in this direction, there is a final peripety in the hero's slaying.

Coriolanus's wife, Virgilia, is quickly "derivable." In contrast with his continual bluster, she is his "gracious silence." Contrasting with his bloodthirsty mother, she faints at the very mention of blood. In her sensitiveness and devotion, she is by implication a vote for Coriolanus. There's a skillful touch, in act 4, scene 2, where she flares up for a moment against the Tribunes, and boasts of her husband as a fighter: "He'ld make an end of thy posterity." There's a different twist, but surely conceived in the spirit of the same theater, when the young son (who is a chip off the old block, and loved to

rip apart a butterfly) flares up at his father. The most notable thing
about Valeria, from the standpoint of Shakespearean dramaturgy, is
the fact that, though this friend of the family serves well for handling
the relation between mother-in-law and daughter, she has a much
less active role in the play than she does in Plutarch. For in Plutarch,
she suggests that the women go to plead with Coriolanus and dissuade him from attacking Rome, whereas the whole musculature of
Shakespeare's play requires maximum stress upon his mother's role
in this development. The two Generals (Titus Lartius and Cominius)
are "derivable" from Coriolanus in the sense that, both being men
of high repute, their constant respect for him speaks for him. Also,
his loyalty to them serves to establish that he is not avid for dictatorial power, but genuinely represents an integral conflict between patricians and plebeians. (Shakespeare's formula for Coriolanus's treatment of the commoners had been summed up by a minor character
thus: "He seeks their hate with greater devotion than they can render
it him.") The citizens have the mixture of distress, resentment, and
instability that enables them to help Coriolanus get into the kind of
quandaries necessary for him to enact his role. As for the Tribunes,
besides their function in making Coriolanus's bluster look admirable
in comparison with their scheming, they serve to carry the play forward by goading him into the rage that leads to his banishment, and
thus eventually (as one thing leads to another) to his death. All told,
in being the kind of characters they are, the other figures help Coriolanus be the kind of character he is; and by their actions at precisely
the times when they do act, they help lead the appointed (or stylis-
tically anointed) victim to the decision required, by the logic of the
plot, for his downfall. He must turn the army away from Rome, and
under conditions that lead step by step to the sacrifice that will permit the purging of the audience.

But we have not yet considered the remarkable function of Menenius. At first glance, one could "derive" him from Coriolanus
only in the sense that he serves as the ideal link between the patrician
and plebeian factions. In this role, along with his loyalty to Coriolanus, he serves particularly well for shaping the audience's sympathies. For though he is a patrician, and frankly shares the prejudices
of his class, the commoners (and the audience) like him. His use in
this regard is of crucial importance to the play when, in act 4, scene
6, a messenger brings the news that Coriolanus is leading an army
against Rome. To the extent that Rome allusively stood for England,

it was not easy to keep the audience sympathetic with a man whose conduct at this point was so close to out-and-out treason (particularly since at so many points in the play he irritates us). But Menenius picks up Cominius's line, placing the blame upon the Tribunes and the people ("O, you have made good work!")—and when two characters of such high repute take this stand, it helps crowd the audience a bit by shifting the emphasis from the *hero's treason* to his *enemies' provocation* (with the bad effects of the provocation being stressed, while the considerations that would justify it were here left unmentioned). The trick was to show the Tribunes and the people regretting their decision to banish Coriolanus rather than to let them review their grounds for the banishment. This is excellent dramaturgic maneuvering—for Shakespeare, as is typical of him, is here working with more complex motives than an audience's simplest responses to patriot and traitor.

But Menenius's "derivation" as a function of Coriolanus's sacrifice contains other notable ingredients. Despite the great contrast between the diplomatic eloquence of the self-styled "humorous patrician" (who is Coriolanus's godfather) and the heavy-footed, grotesquely heroic mouthings of the formally inevitable victim (for one is mellow where the other is raw), Menenius applies almost the same formula to them both. Of himself he says, "What I think, I utter, and spend my malice in my breath." The same readiness with the word he attributes to Coriolanus thus: "His heart's his mouth. / What his breast forges, that his tongue must vent." (War itself, elsewhere in the play, is called "sprightly, waking, audible, and full of vent," an expression that could serve also to describe Coriolanus's invective.)

But whereas Menenius shares Coriolanus's belief in the intrinsic superiority of the patricians, and makes no secret of the fact even when addressing the commoners, his function will be to uphold circumspectly, "reasonably," much the same position that Coriolanus must represent exorbitantly. (I say "must" because his excessiveness is a formal requirement of his role as victim.) Menenius is the only character in the play (except Aufidius's servants) charged with the responsibilities of putting some aspects of this solemn bluster in a comical light.

His early speech likening the body politic to the human body (one of the many themes Shakespeare found in Plutarch, though it was also a standard notion of the times) serves not only to present the attitude of the patricians in the best light (as Coriolanus must present it in the worst). It also sets the conditions for much body imagery throughout the play, particularly images of bodily disease, such as go well with the fact that the body politic is in great disarray. What more relevant than an imagery of bodily diseases in a play dealing with disorders of the body politic? Similarly, since the people are starving, images to do with devouring serve to keep thought of such conditions hovering about the edges of our consciousness. And the many references to animals are so treated as to reinforce the vigorous animality of the underlying situation.

The question of imagery, I submit, should be "derived" thus late in the enterprise. With works of a preponderantly imagistic cast (as in much modern poetry), one might properly *begin* with questions of imagery. But in a drama of this sort, one can most profitably begin with considerations of action and character, afterwards deducing the logic of the imagery from these prior considerations, rather than using imagery as the "way-in."

II

Fundamentally, then, the play exploits to the ends of dramatic entertainment, with corresponding catharsis, the tension intrinsic to a kind of social division, or divisiveness, particularly characteristic of complex societies, but present to some degree in even the simplest modes of living. (I take it that the presence of a priesthood or similar functionaries dealing with things of this world in terms of a "beyond," is on its face evidence that a society is marked by some degree of social differentiation, with corresponding conflicts of interest. And at the very least, even tribes that come closest to a homogeneous way of life are marked by differentiation between the work of men and women or between youth and age.)

This malaise, which affects us all but which in varying degrees and under varying circumstances we attempt to mitigate, is here made insultingly unforgettable. Coriolanus's *hubris* (whether you choose to translate it as "pride" or as "excessiveness") aggravates the situation constantly. And when he dies (after a change of heart that enables us to pity him even while we resent his exaggerated ways of representing our own less admirable susceptibilities, with their corresponding "bad conscience"), he dies as one who has taken on the responsibility and has been appropriately punished. Thereby we are cleansed, thanks to his overstating of our case.

Along with this tension, which is of long duration in societies, we considered the likelihood that, when the play originally appeared, it also exploited a "timely topic," the unrest caused by the Enclosure Acts, when new men of means took over for sheepraising, much land that had traditionally been available to small farmers, and these "legally" dispossessed tenants were in a state of great frustration. Many were starving while the monopolists were being made into patricians. It was a time when many *nouveaux-riches* were being knighted—and as Aristotle points out, it is *new* fortunes that people particularly resent.

An ironic turn of history has endowed this play with a new kind of "timely topic," owing to the vagaries of current dictatorships. But I would incline to contend that this "new immediacy" is more apparent than real. In the first place, Coriolanus isn't a good fit for the contemporary pattern because the frankness of his dislike for the common people would make him wholly incompetent as a rabble-rouser. A modern demagogue might secretly share Coriolanus's prejudices—but he certainly would not advertise the fact as Coriolanus did. His public heart would bleed for the poor, even while he was secretly shipping state funds to a Swiss bank, against the day when his empire would collapse, and he would flee the country, hoping to spend his last years in luxurious retirement on the Riviera. Presumably our nation is always in danger of pouring considerable funds down such ratholes. Thus, I feel that the attempt to present *Coriolanus* in the light of modern conditions can never quite succeed, since these conditions tend rather to conceal than to point up the cultural trends underlying its purgative use of the tension between upper and lower classes. Or should we call it a "tension behind the tension"? I have in mind a situation of this sort:

The Renaissance was particularly exercised by Machiavelli because he so accurately represented the transvaluation of values involved in the rise of nationalism. A transvaluation was called for, because *religion* aimed at *universal* virtues, whereas the virtues of *nationalism* would necessarily be *factional,* insofar as they pitted nation against nation. Conduct viewed as vice from the standpoint of universal religious values might readily be viewed as admirable if it helped some interests prevail over others. This twist greatly exercised Machiavelli. But though (from the universal point of view) nations confront one another as factions, from the standpoint of any one nation factionalism is conceived in a narrower sense, with nationalism itself taking over the role of the universal.

In Shakespeare's day, as so many of his plays indicate, the kind of *family* factionalism that went with feudal relationships was being transformed into the kind of *class* factionalism that would attain its "perfection" (if we may apply that term to so turbulent a development) in the rise of nationalism, with its drive towards the building of the British Empire. And here Shakespeare tackled this particular tangle of motives in a remarkably direct manner, except of course for the kind of "distance" (with corresponding protection) the play got by treating the subject in terms of ancient Rome rather than his contemporary London.

All told, the motivation split into four overlapping loci: nation, class, family, individual. And in *Coriolanus* we witness a remarkably complex simplification of these issues, dramatically translated into terms of action and character.

Individualism may come and go, but there is a compelling sense in which the individual is always basic. The centrality of the nervous system is such that each of us is unique (each man's steak and his particular toothache being his own and no one else's). And even those who are killed *en masse* nonetheless die one by one. Symbolicity (by assigning proper names and attesting to the rights of private ownership) strongly punctuates this physical kind of individuality. And Shakespeare adds his momentous contribution by building so many plays on the "star" system, with a titular role. I think it is safe to say that *Coriolanus* most thoroughly meets this description. Think of such lines as: "O, me alone! Make you a sword of me?" (1.6.); "Alone I fought in your Corioles walls" (1.7.); "Alone I did it." (5.6.)—or his resolve to stand "As if a man were author of himself" (5.3.)—or a Tribune's grudging tribute to him: "He has no equal" (1.1.)—or his own mother's formula: "You are too absolute" (3.2.). And the play backs up such statements by incessantly making him the center of our attention whether he is on the stage or off.

Yet even his name is not his own, but derives from the sacking of a city. And when he is threatening to lead an army against Rome, he does not know himself; and the sympathetic Cominius tells us (5.1.) that he "forbade all names. / He was a kind of nothing, titleless, / Till he had forged himself a name o' th' fire / of burning Rome"—and that's precisely what, in obedience to his mother's pleadings he did not do. (If he had got a new name from the destruction of Rome as he got the name of "Coriolanus" from his victory over Corioli, the preservation of the pattern would have ironically required that in his new identity he be called "Romanus.") Incidentally, the longer one works with this text, the more ingenious Shakespeare's invention seems when, just before Coriolanus is killed, he *apologizes* because he had fallen into a rage: "Pardon me, lords, 'tis the first time ever / I was forced to scold." But he is addressing the *lords* of Antium, not the commoners. Shortly thereafter the Conspirators will shout, "Kill, kill, kill, kill, kill him!" thereby as they slay modifying poor impotent Lear's line, "Then, kill, kill, kill, kill, kill, kill!" (4.6.192).

But such considerations bring us to the next locus of motives, the *familial,* which the play brings to a focus in the "mother, wife, child" formula, used variously by Menenius (5.1.28–29), himself (5.2.78), and Volumnia (5.3.101), hers being the most effective, when she bewails the sight of him for "Making the mother, wife, and child to see / The son, the husband, and the father tearing / His country's bowels out." Yet to say as much is to move us almost as quickly into the realm of *class* and *nation,* since his family identity was so intensely that of a *patrician,* and his individualistic ways of being a patrician had brought him into conflict with all Rome.

Here you confront the true poignancy of his predicament, the formula being: individualistic prowess, made haughty towards the people by mother's training, and naturally unfit for the ways of peaceful persuasion with regard to the citizenry as a whole. The *class* motive comes to a focus terministically in the manipulations that have to do with the key word, "noble." But the *nation* as motive gets its forceful poignancy when the play so sets things up that Coriolanus maneuvers himself and is maneuvered into a situation whereby this individualistic mother-motivated patrician patriot is all set to attack his own country, which at the beginning of the play he had defended with such signal valor, despite his invective against the commoners. As Granville-Barker has well said: "Play and character become truly tragic only when Marcius, to be traitor to Rome, must turn traitor to himself."

Yet, so far as I can see, the treatment of this motivational tangle (individual-family-class-nation) is not in itself "cathartic," unless one uses the term in the Crocean sense rather than the Aristotelian. (That is, I have in mind the kind of relief that results purely from the well-ordered presentation of an entanglement. Such a complexity just *is*. But Shakespeare transforms this motionless knot into terms of an irreversible narrative sequence, the "cure" here residing not in a sacrifice as such, but rather in the feeling of "getting somewhere" by the sheer act of expression, even though the scene centered in conditions when Coriolanus was totally immobilized, a quite unusual state for so outgoing a character.) My soundest evidence for catharsis of this sort (whereby the sheer unfolding of expression can impart a kind of relief to our kind of animal, that lives by locomotion) is the nursery rhyme:

> The grand old Duke of York
> He had ten thousand men
> He marched them up to the top of the hill
> Then he marched them down again.
> And when they were up they were up
> And when they were down they were down
> And when they were only halfway up
> They were neither up nor down.

III

I'm among the company of those who would call *Coriolanus* a "grotesque" tragedy. So our final problem is to make clear just wherein its grotesqueness resides, and how this quality might also contribute to its nature as medicinal.

Obviously, in contrast with the typical sacrificial victims of Greek tragedy, Coriolanus rather resembles a character in a satyr play. He is almost like a throwback to the kind of scurrilities that Aristotle associates with the origins of the tragic iamb, in relation to the traditional meter of lampoons. (See *Poetics* 4.) So some critics have called it a "satiric" tragedy. But "grotesque" seems closer, since Coriolanus is *not* being satirized. The clearest evidence that he is being presented as a *bona fide* hero is the fact that *every* person of good standing in the play admires him or loves him and is loyal to him, despite his excesses. What does all this mean?

Still considering the problem from the standpoint of *tensions* and their exploitation for dramatic effects (that is to say, poetic delight), can we not find another kind of tension exploited here for medicinal purposes? It concerns the function of Coriolanus as a "railer," a master of vituperation. Dramaturgically, such a figure is, at the very least, of service in the sense that, by keeping things stirred up, he enables the dramatist to fish in troubled waters. When a cantankerous character like Coriolanus is on the stage (and Shakespeare turns up many such), there is a categorical guaranty that things will keep on the move. Yet, beyond that sheerly technical convenience (whereby Coriolanus does in one way what Iago does in another, towards keeping a play in motion), there is the possibility that such a role in itself may be curative, as a symbolic remedy for one particular kind of repression typical of most societies.

I might best make my point by quoting some remarks I made elsewhere about another scurrilous tragic victim, Shakespeare's Timon of Athens. There, however, the cut is different. Coriolanus throughout is respectful to the patricians and directs his insults only to the plebeians. But Timon, beginning as a great lover of mankind, ends as a total misanthrope. These paragraphs from my essay on *Timon of Athens* bear upon Timon's possible appeal as vilifier in the absolute:

> *Invective,* I submit, is a primary "freedom of speech," rooted extralinguistically in the helpless rage of an infant that states its attitude by utterances wholly unbridled. In this sense, no mode of expression could be more "radical," unless it be the closely allied motive of sheer *lamentation,* undirected wailing. And perhaps the sounds of contentment which an infant makes, when nursing or when being bedded or fondled, mark the pre-articulate origins of a third basic "freedom," *praise.*
>
> Among these three, if rage is the infantile prototype of invective, it is a kind of "freedom" that must soon be subjected to control, once articulacy develops. For though even praise can get one into trouble (for instance, when one happens to praise A's enemy in the presence of A, who happens also to be both powerful and rancorous); and though lamentation can on occasion be equally embarrassing (if one is heard to lament a situation among persons who favor it), invective most directly invites pugnacity, since it is itself a species of pugnacity.
>
> Obviously, the Shakespearean theater lends itself perfectly to the effects of invective. Coriolanus is an excellent

case in point. Even a reader who might loathe his politics cannot but be engrossed by this man's mouthings. Lear also has a strong measure of such appeal, with his impotent senile maledictions that come quite close to the state of man's equally powerless infantile beginnings. . . . And that delightfully run-down aristocrat, Falstaff, delights us by making a game of such exercises.

Though one has heard much about the repression of sexual motives, in our average dealings invective is the mode of expression most thoroughly repressed. This state of affairs probably contributes considerably to such "cultural" manifestations as the excessive violence on television, and the popular consumption of crude political oratory. Some primitive tribes set aside a special place where an aggrieved party can go and curse the king without fear of punishment (though if our society had such an accommodation, I'm sure there'd be a secret agent hiding behind every bush). In earlier days the gifted railer was considered invaluable by reason of his expert skill at cursing the forces deemed dangerous to the welfare of the tribe (see on this point some interesting data in Robert C. Elliott's book *The Power of Satire: Magic, Ritual, Art,* and above all his suggestive and entertaining appendix on "The Curse"). At the very least, in figures such as Coriolanus we get much of such expressiveness, without the rationale of magic, but under the "controlled conditions" of a drama about political unrest. And if he dies of being so forthright, downright and outright (if not exactly upright), it's what he "deserved." For as regards the *categorical* appeal of invective, it resides not so much in the particular objects inveighed against, but in the sheer process of inveighing. And Coriolanus, like Timon, has given vent with fatal overthoroughness to untoward tendencies which, in our "second nature," we have "naturally" learned to repress.

IV

In conclusion, then, where are we? We have been considering Coriolanus's qualifications as a scapegoat, whose symbolic sacrifice is designed to afford an audience pleasure. We have suggested: (1) His primary role as a cathartic vessel resides in the excessiveness with which he forces us to confront the discriminatory motives intrinsic to society as we know it. (2) There is a sheerly "expressive" kind of catharsis in his way of giving form to the complexities of *family, class,* and *national* motives as they come to a focus in the self-conflicts of an *individual*. (3) There is the "curative" function of invective as such, when thus released under controlled conditions that transform the repressed into the expressed, yet do us no damage. (4) The attempt has been made to consider the "paradox of substance" whereby the chosen scapegoat can "be himself" and arrive at the end "proper to his nature" only if many events and other persons "conspire" to this end, the persons by being exactly the kind of persons they are, and the events by developing in the exact order in which they do develop. To sum it all up, then, in a final formula for tragic catharsis: (a formula I wrote with such a play as *Coriolanus* in mind, though it could be applied *mutatis mutandis* to other texts):

> Take some pervasive unresolved tension typical of a given social order (or of life in general). While maintaining the "thought" of it in its overall importance, reduce it to terms of personal conflict (conflict between friends, or members of the same family). Feature some prominent figure who, in keeping with his character, though possessing admirable qualities, carries this conflict to excess. Put him in a situation that points up the conflict. Surround him with a cluster of characters whose relations to him and to one another help motivate and accentuate his excesses. So arrange the plot that, after a logically motivated turn, his excesses lead necessarily to his downfall. Finally, suggest that his misfortune will be followed by a promise of general peace.

The Polity in *Coriolanus*

Norman Rabkin

Though the politics of *Julius Caesar* is essentially the same as that of the [Henriad], setting visionary idealism against revolutionary *Realpolitik* and making a choice of one or the other a mistake, the Roman play is far more pessimistic. In *Julius Caesar* we find no statements like the Archbishop of Canterbury's portrait of an ideal state, no hint of an ideal polity such as Henry V approaches no matter how temporarily. Moreover, whereas Bolingbroke is a man in whom considerable virtue is merely qualified by the fact that his goal is power as much as the good of the state, Mark Antony's virtues are less easy to perceive, and Octavius, unlike those who triumph in the histories, is a selfish and unprincipled man from whom one can expect only evil. But what makes the politics of *Julius Caesar* hopelessly tragic is Brutus. Richard II is a man undone by vices which Shakespeare makes us understand have their virtuous aspects and would be attractive elsewhere. But Brutus is ruined by his virtues, and they are presented so much as such that many critics have found themselves unable to believe that Shakespeare really wants us to find fault with him. It is Brutus's hope for politics, his belief that reason and will can make history human rather than mechanical, his dream of Rome's good, that destroy him and the kind of world he generously wants. In his attractiveness is the true complementarity of the play. Once again, but more poignantly than in any previous historical play, Shakespeare has created a tragedy in which what we hope of

From *Shakespeare and the Common Understanding.* ©1967 by Norman Rabkin. Free Press, 1967.

the world is poised against what the world really is, and there is no possibility of the kind of world men with ideals and vision can be content with. Never again in a play dealing with history will Shakespeare allow us to believe even for a moment that such a state may exist as Brutus believed in and as Shakespeare himself for the moment of *Henry V* may have thought possible. The tragedy of the historical plays is based increasingly on Shakespeare's psychology, which sees human ideals and the virtue of reason set hopelessly against the fact of the human drive for power. One can understand history and participate actively in politics in the light of the first, *Julius Caesar* tells us, but one will be doomed to failure; or one can succeed by means of an understanding of the other, only to abandon the dream of a commonwealth devoted to the common good.

In his last political play Shakespeare carries the tragic pessimism of *Julius Caesar* to its conclusion. In *Coriolanus* as in the earlier plays he creates a protagonist whose virtues are his vices, whose moral assets disqualify him for political success. But here he goes even further than in *Caesar* to demonstrate that the virtue of the political idealist, though better than any other moral quality evinced in the play, is so self-destructive and so flawed in other ways as hardly to deserve the name virtue. In *Coriolanus* Shakespeare demonstrates bitterly that even the idealism we admired in Brutus is a pipe dream, and in so doing he comes closer than ever before to our least illusioned sense of what political reality may be. No modern dramatist has written a more despairing or a more convincing play about man and the state.

In a grim parody of the opening of *Julius Caesar,* the first scene begins with the passionate charge of a number of mutinous citizens that Caius Marcius, later to be named Coriolanus, is "chief enemy to the people" (1.1.8). Like Othello and Antony, the hero is presented to us first from a hostile point of view, but the initial denunciation of Marcius is even more striking for its prophetic qualities. He is, after all, in the course of very little time, going to become Rome's hero and leader, get himself banished as chief enemy to the people, become what he has been accused of as he joins forces with Rome's enemy, the Volscian Aufidius, and ultimately die violently at the hands of his erstwhile friends. Whether or not the people's charge at the outset is true, however, its moral force is vitiated by their motivations: "Let us kill him, and we'll have corn at our own price. Is 't a verdict?" (1.1.10–11). From here to the end of the play, shortsighted selfishness in those who surround him will be an important part of the moral background against which we shall have to construct our judgments of the hero himself.

The chorus of popular criticism of Marcius reaches its climax in a strange bit of dialogue:

> FIRST CITIZEN: I say unto you, what he hath done
> famously, he did it to that end: though soft-
> conscienced men can be content to say it was for his
> country, he did it to please his mother, and to be
> partly proud; which he is, even to the altitude of his
> virtue.
> SECOND CITIZEN: What he cannot help in his nature, you
> account a vice in him. You must in no way say he is
> covetous.
>
> (1.1.36–44)

The most interesting thing about this description is its judiciousness. The two men agree that Marcius has so many faults that one does not need to accuse him of the selfishness we have already seen the citizens manifesting; and strangely they suggest in their brief comments all the possible interpretations of Marcius's behavior that the play will make available: He is motivated by honor, by the desire for fame, by patriotism, by the desire to please his mother, by pride. Moreover, his pride and his virtues are linked, and his pride can be seen as not so much a vice as a part of his nature that he cannot help, a tic, a neurosis. Again and again as the hero's character unfolds itself to us we shall find our minds returning to this strange mash of incompatible judgments and perceptions. We shall find ourselves disturbed about the relations of moral principle to personal psychology, of virtue and vice in action to inner compulsion in character; and we shall find that, like the character of Mark Antony, that of Caius Marcius grows more rather than less ambivalent before our eyes.

There is nothing ambivalent, however, in the presentation of the populace. Even a Stalinist critic of Shakespeare, who sees *Coriolanus* as reflecting Shakespeare's "profound disillusionment with absolutism, the court, the state officials, and the upper classes" and as a play in which "the plebeians constitute the only positive force," recognizes at least that Shakespeare is disturbed by the "political immaturity" of the people. The populace is consistently presented as unstable, fickle, anarchical, deficient in vision. Our attitude toward them is defined in the first scene by the hero's friend Menenius Agrippa, an easygoing aristocrat who responds to their mutiny by telling his famous fable of the rebellion of the body's members against the belly. Speaking in the traditional metaphor in which the state is a body, organically interdependent, nourished from a single source, Menenius uses the fable to his own ends, and Shakespeare uses it for effects that reach beyond this moment. Menenius's purpose, and the immediate effect of the account, is the degradation of the plebes. If the state is a body, the first citizen is the great toe of the assembly, his fellows mindless members who are fed but contribute nothing to the general welfare. The larger effect is the result of a limitation in Menenius's own vision. The notion of the state as organism is familiar to us from the earlier plays and part of the optimistic Renaissance myth of the state, but Shakespeare has changed the tone of the ancient fable he allows Menenius to tell so that the whole state comes to seem distasteful. The senate, center and source of the state's welfare, is only the belly; the sensual Menenius, who substitutes belly for brain in his own life, would find nothing wrong with such a picture, but the speech, taken as an ideal vision of the nature of the state, is repellent.

It is at this moment, when the populace has presented itself as selfish and utterly contemptible, and the voice of its aristocratic government has shown a good deal of wit but not much vision, that the hero of the tragedy first appears, railing. As Traversi has pointed out, Marcius's entry is a "masterpiece of irony," a "perversion of the traditional speech of warlike heroes." Where we expect uplifting oration, we get rodomontade. If the nobility would lay aside its ruth and let him use his sword, says the military hero of Rome,

> I'd make a quarry
> With thousands of these quarter'd slaves, as high
> As I could pick my lance.
>
> (ll. 202–4)

When word comes that the Volscians are planning war against Rome, General Scrooge rejoices at the opportunity to reduce the surplus population of his city, and sardonically observes that now the Roman plebes can steal Volscian corn: "Take these rats thither / To gnaw their garners" (1.1.253–54).

By the end of the first scene we are bewildered. Though the populace is ugly enough to throw our sympathies to Marcius, his undignified fury cools those sympathies. Unable to determine whose side we are to be on, we may begin to think that this is going to be the kind of play in which not sympathy but mocking contempt is the playwright's aim; that is, we begin to expect that the whole play will be a bitter satire.

The brief second scene makes us wonder, though, as it introduces us to Tullus Aufidius, Marcius's counterpart in the Volscian world. For as we see Aufidius scheming in the Senate at Corioles, planning deception against Rome, objecting because word has got to the Romans that the Volscians are preparing for war, we realize that the one political vice we have not seen in Marcius is a willingness to use policy; he makes no pretense about his feelings. We learn moreover that Aufidius and Marcius are sworn enemies. The play's structure thus leads us to qualify our initial censure of Coriolanus, and to begin to be aware of the central issue.

In the third scene Shakespeare adds to the uneasiness that stems from our inability to decide what judgments to make as we meet Volumnia, the hero's mother:

> I pray, you daughter, sing; or express yourself in a more comfortable sort: if my son were my husband, I should freelier rejoice in that absence wherein he won honour than in the embracements of his bed where he would show most love. When yet he was but tender-bodied and the only son of my womb, when youth with comeliness plucked all gaze his way, when for a day of kings' entreaties a mother should not sell him an hour from her beholding, I, considering how honour would become such a person, that it was no better than picturelike to hang by the wall, if renown made it not stir, was pleased to let him seek danger where he was like to find fame. To a cruel war I sent him; from whence he returned, his brows bound with oak. I tell thee, daughter, I sprang not more in joy at first hearing he was a man-child than now in first seeing he had proved himself a man.
>
> (1.3.1–19)

Surely this speech reflects our ideal vision of Rome. We may carp at Volumnia's insistence that *she sent* her son to a bloody war, but in the mother preferring her son's death to his lack of honor, reflected in the next speech she makes, we recognize the classic Roman matron.

villainous woman is too much the man, the manager, the denier of
her femininity: Tamora; Goneril; Regan; Lady Macbeth, who would
be unsexed, who would pluck her nipple from the boneless gums of
her smiling babe and dash its brains out. The weak woman lacks too
much of man: Olivia, who moons away in a perpetual posture of
ailing emotion; the helpless Ophelia ("I do not know, my lord, what
I should think"); Gertrude; Bianca; Hero; and so on. The ideal
woman in Shakespeare is always utterly feminine in charm and acceptance of her place in the social hierarchy, but equipped with a
masculine will as strong as iron: General Cordelia, the two Portias,
Viola, Rosalind, Beatrice, the matured Juliet, Isabella, Helena, Hotspur's Kate, and Desdemona. Significantly the ideal woman in
Shakespearean comedy often disguises herself as a man, then re-
claims her feminine identity. In *Coriolanus* Volumnia perplexes us at
first. We do not know whether she is presented as ideal or as leaning
too much in the direction of Lady Macbeth; but the presentation of
Virgilia as an ideal type (and we must note the touching genuineness
of her husband's affection for her) tells us how we must ultimately
judge the hero's mother.

At the moment, however, we do not know that our feelings will
eventually be so directed, and toward both Volumnia and her son
they remain ambivalent, as they will through much of this movement of the play. As he has done so often, Shakespeare forces us once
again to see a crucial characterization according to opposing systems
of value. We simultaneously admire and are horrified by Volumnia
and her vision. And so it is with war and soldiery. Marcius has already aroused in us one possible attitude toward war, our sense of its
brutality, its meaninglessness, its ability to degrade the men who
pursue it. But in the next scene we find corroboration for the gallant
and inspiring picture of war suggested earlier by Volumnia's first
speeches, as Marcius and his fellow general Titus Lartius, camped
before Corioles, show us what friendship among men of war can be:
hearty, unaffected, cheerful, laconic, and mutually respectful. This
sense of Marcius's military life and of war becomes more pleasant as,
his tone reminiscent of Henry V, he urges his men enthusiastically to
battle; but it collapses immediately as, his soldiers beaten back, Marcius storms on stage ranting at his men:

> All the contagion of the south light on you,
> You shames of Rome! you herd of——Boils and plagues

> Plaster you o'er, that you may be abhorr'd
> Further than seen and one infect another
> Against the wind a mile!
>
> (1.4.30–34)

Through all the military scenes of the first act we are held poised between our sense of the gallantry of war and our feeling of its hideousness. Let me cite one example of the subtle efficiency with which Shakespeare thus suspends our judgments. The Romans have virtually been defeated; against impossible odds Marcius fights his way back to Cominius's camp, and the two generals select soldiers to accompany Marcius back into the battle he insists on fighting despite his wounds. Cominius asks Marcius to take his choice of the men who will be most useful to him, and Marcius answers:

> Those are they
> That most are willing. If any such be here—
> As it were sin to doubt—that love this painting
> Wherein you see me smear'd; if any fear
> Lesser his person than an ill report;
> If any think brave death outweighs bad life
> And that his country's dearer than himself;
> Let him alone, or so many so minded,
> Wave thus, to express his disposition,
> And follow Marcius.
>
> (1.6.66–75)

Again shades of Henry V at Agincourt. But notice that the love of bloody painting comes first, the love of country last. The opposition Shakespeare has so carefully established between two aspects of the warlike personality reveals the doubleness of our own attitudes toward war, and more particularly the composite nature of that personality. The gallantry is inseparable from the bloodiness; it is not the gentle Cominius but the savage Marcius who has the force to lead his broken troops into victory. But Shakespeare is not, like a sociologist, simply reporting his observations, but rather challenging our moral sensibility. If the character of the soldier is as we see it here, what is its moral status? As the play is set up so far, this is a disturbing and unanswerable question.

Act 1, scene 9 enlarges and changes this question. A crucial scene, it introduces what from the hero's point of view will be the most important question of the play. What we have been asking so far, as we have tried to come to a simple attitude toward Volumnia and her son, is what judgment we are to pass on that classical Rome we recognize in the play. What is Rome, a world of bloody passion and the love of death, or a theater for exemplary heroism? But the question 1.9. presents Marcius is rather, "What is honor?"

Again it is structure—the juxtaposition of scenes—that makes us know what questions Shakespeare wants us to ask. Increasingly through this act Marcius has grown in our esteem as his prowess and manliness have met all tests. In the minuscule eighth scene, which lasts scarcely a minute, we have watched his climactic defeat of Aufidius, which both ends the battle and, equally importantly, reminds us of the opposition between the dishonorable leader of the Volscians and the upright Roman general. And now in scene 9 we find Marcius's superior Cominius offering him the honors he has earned. With the economy characteristic of his maturest plays, Shakespeare simultaneously presents in the terse opening dialogue of this scene a brilliant bit of drama, a tense exchange between two complicated human beings, and an almost abstract argument.

Cominius praises Rome's noblest soldier; Marcius objects mildly but firmly to the praise, which embarasses him no matter who gives it. His reasoning is appropriately modest and his manner gracious:

> I have done
> As you have done; that's what I can; induced
> As you have been; that's for my country:
> He that has but effected his good will
> Hath overta'en mine act.
>
> (ll.15–19)

But Cominius can answer Marcius on his own grounds: If it is Rome he is interested in, it is for Rome's benefit that Marcius must accept praise:

> You shall not be
> The grave of your deserving; Rome must know
> The value of her own: 'twere a concealment
> Worse than a theft, no less than a traducement,
> To hide your doings.
>
> (1.9.19–23)

Marcius does not attempt to answer this argument, remarking only that his wounds hurt when they are talked about; Cominius replies that they would hurt worse if ingratitude were their reward, and signals his estimation of Marcius's services' worth by offering him the tenth part of the spoils taken, and at this point the action erupts. "I thank you, general," the hero says, "But cannot make my heart consent to take / A bribe to pay my sword." A flourish sounds, the army cheers, "Marcius, Marcius," and throws up caps and lances—and Marcius denounces the entire gathering as flatterers and hypocrites.

> You shout me forth
> In acclamations hyperbolical;
> As if I loved my little should be dieted
> In praises sauced with lies.
>
> (1.9.50–53)

This is a peculiar performance. Modesty and self-respecting dignity are one thing, but the gratuitous insulting of his friend and benefactor as a briber and of the army he has led to victory as a pack of liars is another. What is most peculiar is what Cominius observes in calmly ignoring the insult and answering his difficult protégé: In rejecting the offered honors Marcius is damaging the good report that he has earned.

And now, at this crucial impasse, Shakespeare gives us the most dramatic example of a device he has used elsewhere: He makes an issue of his hero's name in order to make us think about the problem of the hero's identity. Just so in *Troilus and Cressida,* as we have seen [elsewhere], the questions are explicitly and repeatedly asked: What is Cressid? Who is Troilus? And in *Antony and Cleopatra,* troubled by the two possible judgments between which we are suspended, we hear constantly: "Antony will be himself"; "Sometimes, when he is not Antony"; "Name Cleopatra as she is called in Rome"; "Had our general been what he knew himself, it had gone well"; "Observe how Antony becomes his flaw"; "I am Antony yet"; "What's her name / Since she was called Cleopatra?"; "But since my lord is Antony again, I will be Cleopatra." But here history allows Shakespeare to do what he could not do elsewhere, actually to change the name of his character on the stage. From now on, since Marcius will accept no other rewards, Cominius announces he will be called Coriolanus, the conqueror of Corioles. Marcius accepts without protest; his new identity is defined—like the identity of all Shakespearean heroes, we might note—by his achievement.

But the meaning of the name is ambiguous, and does not solve the debate which underlies the quarrel between Marcius and Cominius. For there is a real issue there, making sense of what otherwise would be quirky perversity in the hero. For Cominius, and for the army so eager that their hero accept their gifts, honor is something that comes to one for one's achievement in the world; it is conferred by society, involved in good name and reputation, public praise and office; the unrewarded deed is the grave of its deserving. For Caius Marcius, however, the deed is its own reward, honorable or dishonorable regardless of what people think of it; honor is a quality of action, not of action's effects; honest praise is flattery and lies because all words that describe what is ultimately personal and subjective must miss the point. As we shall discover later, Marcius feels special justification in his position because he feels those who would "honor" him to be so unworthy, but he rejects accolades even from the worthy Cominius; the argument is philosophical.

As he had done in *Henry IV,* Shakespeare is exploring the double implications of a word on which are built some of our most important ethical and social structures. Shakespeare did not invent the problem, nor did it end with his plays. E. R. Dodds and Bruno Snell, among others, have demonstrated in their brilliant studies of the development of Greek religious concepts that Greek thought fluctuated from prephilosophical times between the Homeric assumption that virtue is defined by and consists in a certain kind of social approval and the later idea of an internalized virtue responsible only to absolutes that lie beyond social jurisdiction. An interesting history of the west might be written from the point of view of our culture's inability to determine finally whether it is what anthropologists call a shame culture, based on an intense sensitivity to communal standards, or a guilt culture, in which individual conscience and consciousness are the only standards the virtuous man can respect. It is not surprising that the Renaissance, that age in which the syncretism of western culture was felt most urgently and in which much that is important in philosophy, statecraft, and the arts was the result of an often conscious tension between Hebrew-Christian and classical elements, should have produced so many literary works in which the idea of honor in its opposed meanings is crucial. The ambiguity of the idea, classically developed in the implicit debate be-

tween Hotspur and Falstaff, is crucial as well in numerous plays by
Shakespeare's contemporaries, and by the mid-seventeenth century
has become one of the few subjects left to tragedy. Nor does it fail
to trouble subsequent ages. I have argued elsewhere that the meaning
of Richardson's *Clarissa* is its author's understanding of the process
by which the shame-culture idea of honor, the idea that virtue and
social approval are identical, has itself become internalized in his
heroine so that it has the force of the guilt-culture idea. For the
middle-class eighteenth-century heroine social propriety and con-
vention are sacred virtues; her "'character'"—a word ambiguous
precisely as "honor" is ambiguous—is "'more valuable . . . than my
life.'" The problem still occupies us; statesmen find themselves
caught in the trap of our "national honor," unable to determine
whether by it they mean our commitment to certain inviolable political ideals or what other nations think of us; and an interesting bit
of material for the cultural history of our time is the formula of firms
admonishing clients for whom they have opened charge accounts,
"Your credit rating is a sacred trust." In *Coriolanus* Shakespeare
comes most to grips with the problem that has troubled his treatment of politics from the beginning: the problem of honor.

In accepting the name Coriolanus, Marcius accepts public recognition for what he has done, and necessarily compromises himself. Like Lear, Macbeth, Brutus, and Hamlet, Coriolanus makes us
realize here how much the hero is created by what he has accomplished, defined by the events through which he has passed. And
perhaps in accepting his new name Coriolanus realizes, as certainly
those do who give him the name and we do who watch the cere-
mony, that the world is not quite so subjective as Marcius had
thought. Most of the events in which we are involved include other
people; Coriolanus's name memorializes a public battle and, like all
names, is given *to* him; the achievement recorded by the new name
is an achievement whose meaning derives from the fact that it was
performed for Rome. Coriolanus cannot both insist on the private-
ness of his action and act as a public leader in a public cause. The
moral problem suggested by the ambiguity of "honor" here seems
already to be resolved; yet we will find it becoming more acute as
the play continues.

Coriolanus has acted somewhat churlishly in this scene; whatever the principle according to which he justifies his action, his manner to Cominius and the rest is unwarrantedly unpleasant, and one

suspects at its root a social awkwardness of which we shall see a good deal later. At the end of the scene we are left primarily with a sense of ineptness. Coriolanus gallantly asks that a poor man who gave him quarters and assistance be given his freedom, then realizes he doesn't remember the man's name and can't return his kindness. But whatever we hold against the Coriolanus we have come to know in the first act, our meeting with Aufidius in the tenth and last scene of the act reminds us of Coriolanus's unique virtues: Aufidius too is concerned with honor, but only as an impulse to put out of the way in order to get what he wants, and he self-consciously disavows the course of honor, boasting to his cronies that if wrath will not destroy Marcius then craft will.

I have gone through the first act serially because in it Shakespeare so carefully establishes the problem that will generate the entire play. The world of the tragedy is set in motion at the moment Marcius becomes Coriolanus and Aufidius declares his true colors to us, and immediately the problems we have merely sensed underlying the earlier action burst into crisis. Returned to peace, Coriolanus is summoned to the Capitol, where, to the surprise of no one, the Senate offers him the consulship. Only one formality must be observed: To mark ceremonially the role of the people in the choice of their leader, Coriolanus must go through the motions of a popular campaign, showing the citizens his wounds, wearing the gown of humility. And so a group of citizens gathers at the Forum to put their hero through his performance. Though somewhat uneasy because of his former contempt for them, they are comically smug and benevolent as they make preparations to grant the great man their largesse.

> Here he comes, and in the gown of humility: mark his behaviour. We are not to stay all together, but to come by him where he stands, by ones, by twos, and by threes. He's to make his requests by particulars; wherein everyone of us has a single honour, in giving him our own voices with our own tongues: therefore follow me, and I'll direct you how you shall go by him.
>
> (2.3.44–51)

In the situation Shakespeare has taken from Plutarch he finds a vehicle for a political question as relevant to our democratic society as to Roman democracy, the question in fact that John F. Kennedy

asked in *Profiles in Courage:* What is the role of the man of principle
in politics? Can he act, involve himself in the world, and retain his
honor? Can he uncompromisingly stand by his principles and yet be
a force in the world? Or, if he must compromise his principles in
order to gain the popular support he needs to give him force, can
those principles remain operative? The passage just cited ironically
suggests Coriolanus's grounds for refusing to concede anything to
popular will. Each of the citizens has a single honor to confer; honor
is what comes to the man who deserves it; it is given by voices; it is
thus at least as much the reflection of those who confer it as of him
who receives it. We already know what Coriolanus would say to
such a definition of honor, and he does not disappoint us. His tone
at first is one of bitter mockery as he realizes how neatly the situation
sets his required role against his political philosophy:

> What must I say?
> "I pray, sir,"—Plague upon't! I cannot bring
> My tongue to such a pace:—"Look, sir, my wounds!
> I got them in my country's service, when
> Some certain of your brethren roar'd and ran
> From the noise of our own drums."
>
> (2.3.55–60)

Disregarding Menenius's cagy advice to avoid mentioning his con-
stituents' cowardice, Coriolanus continues to mock them, and finally performs his assignment only by casting his requests in an
ironic mold which the citizens, though it makes them nervous, are
unable to understand and reject. All that the candidate asks is all that
he thinks them capable of giving him: their *voices.* The word, which
occurs an astonishing forty-one times in the play, is sounded no less
than twenty-four times in this scene, until we come around to the
hero's point of view in which the people *are* merely *voices.* Like Menenius's fable of the belly, Coriolanus's image for the citizens denies
them the power of reason, reducing them to the willful expression
of worthless opinions. Uneasily awed by his haughtiness, the populace assents to the election of its new consul.

   Thus, searching for a way to accept public office in a democracy
without compromising his honor, Coriolanus has chosen the way of
absolute allegiance to his ideals. If Shakespeare wants us to think that
the hero has made the right choice, he nevertheless makes us see the
disastrous results of that choice. In the first place, the unscrupulous

tribunes have no trouble in capitalizing on the people's vague sense that their consul-elect does not like them, and soon they have whipped the rabble up to a rebellion. The only solution is that Coriolanus must once again go hat in hand to his electors, and this time show the wounds he has received in their behalf. Driven on by the pleas of Menenius and Volumnia and by arguments that he must serve the common good, Coriolanus agrees to perform, but knowing their man the tribunes easily goad him to public display of such fury that in one moment he ends his political career in Rome. This turn of events is as much Coriolanus's choice as it is that of his opponents. It is not merely that he is unwilling to compromise, but that the society for which he would have to compromise is not worth serving. Thus Rome banishes him; but from his own point of view Coriolanus banishes the city (3.3.123). "My birth-place hate I," he will say shortly at the gates of Aufidius's home, "and my love's upon / This enemy town" (4.4.23–24).

Rome is an idea for Coriolanus, the idea of honor, and paradoxically that idea has led him to reject the state which had been its avatar. With increasing painfulness for the audience, Shakespeare explores the implications of this paradox as the play moves toward its bitter end. His honor drives the only honorable man in Rome to treachery, to the betrayal of the state with whom not only his fortunes but also his values are inextricably associated. The process means the destruction of the man. Having accepted his identity and his name as Rome's defender, he must now reject that identity until nothing is left but his ever more intense sense of personal honor and a consuming hatred for what he takes to be the source of his humiliation. "Coriolanus / He would not answer to," reports Cominius after an unsuccessful embassy to his old friend;

> forbade all names;
> He was a kind of nothing, titleless,
> Till he had forged himself a name o' the fire
> Of burning Rome.
>
> (5.1.11–14)

And the hero cannot reach his final destruction without learning from the mother who has instilled his virtue and his passion in him the meaning of his action.

> Thou know'st, great son,
> The end of war's uncertain, but this certain,

That, if thou conquer Rome, the benefit
Which thou shalt thereby reap is such a name,
Whose repetition will be dogg'd with curses;
Whose chronicle thus writ: "The man was noble,
But with his last attempt he wiped it out;
Destroy'd his country, and his name remains
To the ensuing age abhorr'd." Speak to me, son:
Thou hast affected the fine strains of honour,
To imitate the graces of the gods.

(5.3.140–50)

Defining his entire life in terms of his inner principle of integrity, Caius Marcius Coriolanus has destroyed his very identity.

The hero's choice, then, whatever its merits, does not work in the world of the play. But what is the alternative to it? Almost schematically, Shakespeare offers a range of possibilities—and none of them is any better. In the first place there is the way taken by Aufidius and the tribunes, a callous and utterly unprincipled opportunism. Sicinius and Brutus regard the events of the world only in terms of what they will bring; spokesmen of the people, they hate those they represent as much as Coriolanus does, yet hypocritically pretend class loyalty in order to acquire personal power. Aufidius's behavior is somewhat more respectable because at least it is based on a kind of principle, the belief that principles have no force in the world. Thus, shrewdly analyzing Coriolanus's political failure—like the citizen at the beginning of the play, he offers a number of psychological and moral causes for the hero's behavior—Aufidius enunciates his own credo:

So our virtues
Lie in the interpretation of the time;
And power, unto itself most commendable,
Hath not a tomb so evident as a chair
To extol what it hath done.
One fire drives out one fire; one nail, one nail;
Rights by rights falter, strengths by strengths do fail.

(4.7.49–55)

Shakespeare does not ask us to decide on the basis of abstract principles that Aufidian *Realpolitik* is wrong; rather, he destroys any sympathy with Aufidius we may have by letting us watch the Volscian cruelly betray Coriolanus while pretending the most intense friendship for him.

But other alternatives seem more attractive. "All's well," says Menenius to the tribunes after the banishment, "and might have been much better, if / He could have temporized" (4.6.16–17). Does Shakespeare suggest compromise, paying the world its due, as a rational course of behavior in contrast to that taken by Coriolanus? Ultimately, we must note, it is Coriolanus's decision to compromise that destroys him. Three likable characters are temporizers: Cominius, Menenius, and Volumnia. None of them will do. Cominius is gracious, noble, civilized, and generous, but he needs Marcius to win his battles for him. In times of crisis societies respond only to the leadership of the passionately committed; Cominius has insufficient vision to take Rome to greatness. Menenius is amiable enough. His notion of social responsibility entails taking all reasonable precautions to insure that he and his fellows will not be driven from the club where they drink their after-dinner port and speak with disarming deprecation of themselves. To charge that his only principle is that one should not rock the boat is to do him an injustice, for Menenius bases his justification of society on a sense of the value of civilization and comfort so pervading that he never feels the need to formulate it. But Menenius's comfortable dream, though it seems in the hour of security and stability to embody vast political power, is insubstantial; it is parasitic, living off the wealth of an established state. Perhaps it is significant that Menenius's thoughts turn constantly to eating, that he can interpret Coriolanus's behavior only by speculating that Coriolanus is hungry. Even the Coriolanuses of the world are glad that it has room for such men as Menenius, and the genuine friendship between the two patricians is touching; but Menenius is a by-product, not an end, and his way of life is no answer to the problems built into the ethical structure of the universe of *Coriolanus*. And finally there is Volumnia. For the Roman matriarch Rome comes first, and she has raised her son as an offering to it. But Rome for Volumnia is not, as it is for Marcius, an abstract ethical idea, but a city, a people, a state, a history. For Rome anything can be sacrificed, and always in honor:

> I would dissemble with my nature where
> My fortunes and my friends at stake required
> I should do so in honour.

(3.2.62–64)

Honor is her theme as it is her son's. But we have seen from the beginning that for Volumnia honor is the glory that Rome can confer on its loyal servants, and that honor can therefore employ policy, political expediency. Her notion of honor is the most tempting alternative to Marcius's idea, but finally it, too, is unsatisfactory. Volumnia's honor requires that Coriolanus violate his sworn word to the Volscians in order to give up the battle against Rome. It demands that Coriolanus see his virtue not in terms of what he has accomplished, but in terms of what it can get him. It concedes that value is dictated not by the nature of the object but by the tastes of the valuer, so that Coriolanus is honorable not so much when he rescues Rome as when he receives the accolades of its worthless citizens.

In fact, the play allows no alternative to Coriolanus's understanding of glory. What does it mean to strive for the recognition of those whose recognition is meaningless—fickle, corruptible, emotional, selfish people held in contempt even by their own tribunes? From the beginning to the end of this somber story the populace is concerned only with what it gets for itself. If, as the tribunes argue, the city is no more than the people, it is scarcely worth the efforts of a Coriolanus. The only leader they will accept is one who is willing and able to tailor himself to fit their need for a leader with the proper image, with the wounds he has earned for them still bleeding and scarcely covered by a tattered garment. The citizens know it is a game they are asking Coriolanus to play, but his willingness to play the game would tell them that he is their man. Do we really want Coriolanus to play the game? In our own world we are all too familiar with the nightmare situation in which the leaders and the led willingly agree on the self-flattery and the self-deception involved in the myth of the state in which they live, and which will collapse the moment it is put to the test because image must ultimately yield to reality. There is a good deal to be said for the man of vision who will not compromise because he recognizes that in the act of compromise itself one can destroy the very object one wants to save.

Nevertheless, Coriolanus's refusal is every bit as destructive. Shakespeare offers us two alternatives, the idea of the state as unbending moral imperative and the idea of the state as a community organized for the benefit of its members—on the one hand, the state as worthy of allegiance only when it represents the highest moral ideals; on the other, "my country right or wrong." And he seems to be telling us hopelessly that neither of these notions of the state will work. The problem is not just that of democracy (which could not in itself have been a burning issue to Shakespeare in 1608), but of the ethical status of the body politic itself.

The question of the radically opposed senses of the word "honor" recurs increasingly in the drama of the early seventeenth century until by the time of the outbreak of civil war in 1642 it has become the main theme of almost all serious plays. This is not surprising in an age in which, as in ours, all is called into question. But Shakespeare is concerned with more than an abstract moral issue; or rather, he recognizes that abstract moral issues are crucial in life because they touch our inner lives, and those inner lives are not computers into which propositions are fed at one end so that syllogistic conclusions can come out at the other. Rather as imaginative literature in general and Shakespeare in particular constantly teach us, we are enormously complicated creatures, and our ideas, whatever their validity and truth, are the product of the most tortuous complex of psychological drives, inexplicable impulses, desires, tastes, and quirks. Often in my account of the hero's behavior I have simplified events by describing them in terms of his rationale, implying that Coriolanus has consciously and coolly chosen the way of honor and that he acts according to a code. In a very important sense this is true, but it is far from being the whole story. As the citizens' descriptions suggested at the beginning of the play, Coriolanus's behavior has a number of causes. He believes in honor as a principle, but perhaps he does so because he has to. Least important, but unmistakable among the forces that shape his behavior, is Marcius's social ineptness. He does not know how to accept praise or to demonstrate gratitude. The only times at which we see him fully at ease and unselfconscious are a few fleeting moments between battles when he is a man among men he trusts, or with his family. Otherwise he can all too easily insult his friends and infuriate his enemies when he has no intention of doing so; a man more socially adept might understand and detachedly put up with the rituals through which society functions, while Coriolanus, unable to perform them gracefully, rejects them furiously. Of this gaucherie Marcius makes a principle too, priding himself on his rocky harshness, his freedom from corrupting social smoothness; but the behavior seems rooted more deeply than the attitude toward it. The second element in the complex of Coriolanus's character is his pride. One character after another, friend or enemy, points out how godlike the man's aspirations and self-image are. In this Coriolanus is not unlike certain intractable political figures of our own day, whose dignity brooks no contradiction, in whom magnificence is as much a matter of personality as it is of principle. Third is his brutality, the quality that makes Marcius a born warrior: "Death, that dark spirit, in's nervy arm doth lie; / Which, being advanced, declines, and then men die" (2.1.177–78). As we have already seen, the attitude which Shakespeare determines in us toward this quality is as ambivalent as our attitude toward his idea of honor. We admire it as the only possible nature for a man called on to accomplish what he must, but fear it as inimical to civilization.

Finally, and most painfully, we recognize the part played in Coriolanus's life by his relation to his mother. She is unmistakably the source of his values, though paradoxically he has learned to love honor and Rome with a totally different understanding from hers of what they mean. (Shakespeare is always skeptical of the success of plans: You may bring up your son to exemplify all that you believe in only to discover that you have succeeded in creating an opponent to your values.) Twice in the play Coriolanus is forced to realize that his passion for honor is merely a lesson badly learned from Volumnia. To see it only as such would be more cynical than Shakespeare teaches us to be; the duality of Coriolanus's motivation in character and principle does not vitiate the principles in which the hero genuinely believes; all men have reasons for believing what they believe. But to Marcius himself it is a shock to realize that he has betrayed the Roman faith of his mother which he had thought he was emulating and gratifying; and once he makes the concession (which Volumnia maneuvers with great sublety and skill), he recognizes the ambiguity of his position. Each time, he yields to Volumnia: first to agree to submit himself once more to popular judgment, second to betray his new Volscian allies. Each time he gives up his own principle for Volumnia, and each time the result is disaster. Perhaps nothing in Shakespeare is more mortifying than Coriolanus's collapse before his mother's will:

> O my mother, mother! O!
> You have won a happy victory to Rome;
> But, for your son,—believe it, O, believe it,
> Most dangerously you have with him prevail'd,
> If not most mortal to him. But, let it come.
> Aufidius, though I cannot make true wars,

> I'll frame convenient peace. Now, good Aufidius,
> Were you in my stead, would you have heard
> A mother less? Or granted less, Aufidius?
>
> (5.3.185–93)

What makes Volumnia twice successful in shifting Coriolanus's course when Cominius, Menenius, and the rest consistently fail is her ability to make her son doubt the integrity of his own faith. If she taught it to him, and if from her point of view he has not got it right, then he cannot have that godlike sense of his own power and independence; in granting Volumnia a favor he is broken as banishment from Rome and military defeat could never have broken him. He would rather not know that the source of his behavior lies in character rather than rational principle.

It is Shakespeare's demonstration of the dominance of character over what we would like to be, of the priority of personality over principle in the motivation of human action, that brings this play as close to being a depressing experience as any tragedy of Shakespeare ever gets. Fighting against the Volscians, haranguing the plebians, justifying his life on philosophical grounds, Coriolanus impresses us as a rare man of principle. But when we see him listening to his mother's reminder that he is the best of her flesh; when we see him struggling hopelessly against the impulses of a loving son; and when we watch him, as he holds Volumnia's hand, surrendering to her all that he has been defending, we realize what power a personal bond possesses, how little one really knows of one's own motivations. And it may occur to us that much of what we have ascribed to Marcius's high principles—his intense idealism, his quick temper, his passionate self-righteousness, his refusal to make accommodating concessions, his lack of concern with physical comfort—may just as well be a function of the fact that he is still hardly more than a boy. Having dismayed us with the suggestion that principle—the only way to live admirably—must lead to ruin, Shakespeare will not allow us to find consolation in the thought that defeated principle at least has its integrity, but rather makes us wonder if we can properly admire what is itself a conditioned result rather than a freely chosen cause.

The inevitability of Coriolanus's fate may not be any more striking than that of other Shakespearean heroes, but because it is based on unmistakable and insuperable qualities of character rather than on such an atmosphere of universal fatality as permeates *King Lear* or

Hamlet, it seems more ineluctable, more immediately confining. Not just Coriolanus, but Menenius and Volumnia, Aufidius and Sicinius and Brutus seem immutable, determined by social and psychological forces over which they have no control. In no other tragedy of Shakespeare is there so little growth and change in character. The sense that man is determined by what is given to him, that little or no room is left for the always elusive but clearly discernible freedom of the other tragic heroes, may be Shakespeare's response to a growing strain in contemporary ethical and psychological speculation. It is not a permanent attitude, at any rate. In *Antony and Cleopatra* the implication is strong that Antony chooses his own destiny: He decides to fight at sea, to follow Cleopatra at Actium, to identify himself with Egypt rather than Rome; and in giving us the impression that he is a free agent, accountable for his actions, Antony reveals his kinship with other tragic heroes in Shakespeare. Not so with Coriolanus.

But in a larger sense *Coriolanus* typifies and carries to an extreme the familiar pattern of Shakespearean tragedy. The hero's virtue—his passionate sense of honor and allegiance to principles—is also his vice. It makes him incomparably better than anyone else in the play and paradoxically worse by the end than all the others. He is the only man whose principles are presented as worthy of respect; he is also, out of love for the idea of Rome, the man who, as Volumnia points out (5.3.114ff.), must either be led through the streets of his Rome as a foreign traitor or "bear the palm for having bravely shed / Thy wife and children's blood." Because of the abstraction with which the ideas are often presented, the paradoxes of the tragic hero and of Shakespeare's dismayed awareness of the nature and role and fate of moral goodness in the world seem more acute here than anywhere else. Coriolanus carries virtue and vice as far as they can go, and almost parodies the Shakespearean identification of the one with the other. In Brutus and Hotspur honor has led the honorable man to dishonor, but nowhere does the dishonor seem so great as at the end of *Coriolanus,* when even the expected reconstruction of the tragic hero in the play's final speeches turns into bitterness and mockery. By the end we know that rational and humane order cannot really be restored because it cannot exist in society. There are no more heroic virtues to learn. Shakespeare has embarked on a new kind of tragedy. Unlike Hamlet, Coriolanus brings down with him all hope of a society that embodies his vision; no catharsis is possible.

If *Coriolanus* thus reaches the limits of Shakespeare's tragic universe, it similarly provides a fit conclusion to his career as composer of plays about history. For here, focusing on the essential problems that sometimes seem to get lost amid the richness and bustle of the earlier history plays, he makes us understand most fully the tragic complementarity of all solutions to the political world he sees. In *Coriolanus* both idealism and grubby reality are subjected to their most searching examination, and the result, perhaps the grimmest play in the canon, brings us to the full understanding of the world of Shakespeare's politics.

"Anger's My Meat": Feeding, Dependency, and Aggression in *Coriolanus*

Janet Adelman

Coriolanus was written during a period of rising corn prices and the accompanying fear of famine: rising prices reached a climax in 1608. In May 1607, "a great number of common persons"—up to five thousand, Stow tells us in his *Annals*—assembled in various Midlands counties, including Shakespeare's own county of Warwickshire, to protest against the acceleration of enclosures and the resulting food shortages. It must have been disturbing to property owners to hear that the rioters were well received by local inhabitants, who brought them food and shovels; doubly disturbing if they were aware that this was one of England's first purely popular riots, unlike the riots of the preceding century in that the anger of the common people was not being manipulated by rebellious aristocrats or religious factions. The poor rioters were quickly dispersed, but— if *Coriolanus* is any indication—the fears that they aroused were not. In fact, Shakespeare shapes his material from the start in order to exacerbate these fears in his audience. In Plutarch the people riot because the Senate refuses to control usury; in Shakespeare they riot because they are hungry. Furthermore, the relentlessly vertical imagery of the play reflects the specific threat posed by this contemporary uprising: in a society so hierarchical—that is, so vertical—as theirs, the rioters' threat to level enclosures implied more than the

From *Shakespeare, Pattern of Excelling Nature,* edited by David Bevington and Jay L. Halio. ©1978 by Associated University Presses, Inc. Associated University Presses, Inc., 1978.

casting down of particular hedges; it seemed to promise a flattening of the whole society. Nor is Shakespeare's exacerbation of these fears merely a dramatist's trick to catch the attention of his audience from the start, or a seventeenth-century nod toward political relevance: for the dominant issues of the uprising—the threat of starvation and the consequent attempt to level enclosures—are reflected not only in the political but also in the intrapsychic world of *Coriolanus;* taken together, they suggest the concerns that shape the play and particularly the progress of its hero.

The uprising of the people at the start of the play points us toward an underlying fantasy in which political and psychological fears come together in a way that can only make each more intense and hence more threatening. For the political leveling promised by the contemporary uprising takes on overtones of sexual threat early in Shakespeare's play: the rising of the people becomes suggestively phallic; and the fear of leveling becomes ultimately a fear of losing one's potency in all spheres. In Menenius's belly fable, the people are "th' discontented members, the mutinous parts," and "the mutinous members" (1.1.110, 148): an audience for whom the mutiny of the specifically sexual member was traditionally one of the signs of the Fall, and for whom the crowd was traditionally associated with dangerous passion, would be prone to hear in Menenius's characterization of the crowd a reference to a part other than the great toe (1.1.154). In this fantasy the hitherto docile sons suddenly threaten to rise up against their fathers, the Senators (1.1.76); and it is characteristic of *Coriolanus* that the contested issue in this Oedipal rebellion is food. The uprising of the crowd is in fact presented in terms that suggest the transformation of hunger into phallic aggression, a transformation that is, as I shall later argue, central to the character of Coriolanus himself: when the first citizen tells Menenius "They say poor suitors have strong breaths: they shall know we have strong arms too" (1.1.58–60), his image of importunate mouths suddenly armed in rebellion suggests the source of Coriolanus's rebellion no less than his own.

If the specter of a multitude of hungry mouths, ready to rise and demand their own, is the exciting cause of *Coriolanus,* the image of the mother who has not fed her children enough is at its center. One does not need the help of a psychoanalytic approach to notice that Volumnia is not a nourishing mother. Her attitude toward food is nicely summed up when she rejects Menenius's invitation to a consolatory dinner after Coriolanus's banishment: "Anger's my meat: I sup upon myself / And so shall starve with feeding" (4.2.50–51). We might suspect her of having been as niggardly in providing food for her son as she is for herself, or rather suspect her of insisting that he too be self-sufficient, that he feed only on his own anger; and indeed, she has apparently fed him only valiantness ("Thy valiantness was mine, thou suck'st it from me" [3.2.129]). He certainly has not been fed the milk of human kindness: when Menenius later tells us that "there is no more mercy in him than there is milk in a male tiger" (5.4.28–29), he seems to associate Coriolanus's lack of humanity not only with the absence of any nurturing female element in him but also with the absence of mother's milk itself. Volumnia takes some pride in the creation of her son, and when we first meet her, she tells us exactly how she's done it: by sending him to a cruel war at an age when a mother should not be willing to allow a son out of the protective maternal circle for an hour (1.3.5–15). She elaborates her creation as she imagines herself mother to twelve sons and then kills all but one of them off: "I had rather had eleven die nobly for their country, than one voluptuously surfeit out of action" (1.3.24–25). To be noble is to die; to live is to be ignoble and to eat too much. If you are Volumnia's son, the choice is clear.

But the most telling—certainly the most disturbing—revelation of Volumnia's attitude toward feeding comes some twenty lines later, when she is encouraging Virgilia to share her own glee in the thought of Coriolanus's wounds: "The breasts of Hecuba / When she did suckle Hector, look'd not lovelier / Than Hector's forehead when it spit forth blood / At Grecian sword contemning" (1.3.40–43). Blood is more beautiful than milk, the wound than the breast, warfare than peaceful feeding. But this image is more disturbing than these easy comparatives suggest. It does not bode well for Coriolanus that the heroic Hector doesn't stand a chance in Volumnia's imagination: he is transformed immediately from infantile feeding mouth to bleeding wound. For the unspoken mediator between breast and wound is the infant's mouth: in this imagistic transformation, to feed is to be wounded; the mouth becomes the wound, the breast the sword. The metaphoric process suggests the psychological fact that is, I think, at the center of the play: the taking in of food is the primary acknowledgment of one's dependence on the world, and as such, it is the primary token of one's vulnerability. But at the same time as Volumnia's image suggests the vulnerability inherent in feeding, it also suggests a way to fend off that vulnerability. In her image, feeding, incorporating, is transformed into spitting out, an aggressive expelling; the wound in turn becomes the mouth that spits "forth blood / At Grecian sword contemning." The wound spitting blood thus becomes not a sign of vulnerability but an instrument of attack.

Volumnia's attitudes toward feeding and dependence are echoed perfectly in her son. Coriolanus persistently regards food as poisonous (1.1.177–78, 3.1.155–56); the only thing he can imagine nourishing is rebellion (3.1.68–69, 116). Only Menenius among the patricians is associated with the ordinary consumption of food and wine without an allaying drop of Tiber in it; and his distance from Coriolanus can be measured partly by his pathetic conviction that Coriolanus will be malleable—that he will have a "suppler" soul (5.1.55)—after he has had a full meal. But for Coriolanus, as for his mother, nobility consists precisely in *not* eating: he twice imagines himself starving himself honorably to death before asking for food, or anything else, from the plebeians (2.3.112–13; 3.3.89–91). And the transformations in mode implicit in Volumnia's image—from feeding to warfare, from vulnerability to aggressive attack, from incorporation to spitting out—are at the center of Coriolanus's character and of our responses to him: for the whole of his masculine identity depends on his transformation of his vulnerability into an instrument of attack, as Menenius suggests when he tells us that each of Coriolanus's wounds "was an enemy's grave" (2.1.154–55). Cominius reports that Coriolanus entered his first battle a sexually indefinite thing, a boy or Amazon (2.2.91), and found his manhood there: "When he might act the woman in the scene, / He prov'd best man i'th' field" (2.2.96–97). The rigid masculinity that Coriolanus finds in war becomes a defense against acknowledgment of his neediness; he attempts to transform himself from a vulnerable human creature into a grotesquely invulnerable and isolated thing. His body becomes his armor (1.3.35, 1.4.24); he himself becomes a weapon "who sensibly outdares his senseless sword, / And when it bows, stand'st up" (1.4.53–54), or he becomes the sword itself: "O me alone! Make you a sword of me!" (1.6.76). And his whole life becomes a kind of phallic exhibitionism, devoted to disproving the possibility that he is vulnerable. Anger becomes his meat as well as his mother's: Volumnia's phrase suggests his mode of defending himself against vulnerability, and at the same time reveals the source of his anger in the deprivation imposed by his mother. We see the quality of his hunger and its transformation when, after his expulsion from Rome, he reminds Aufidius that he has "drawn tuns of blood out of thy country's breast" (4.5.100). Fighting here, as elsewhere in the play, is a poorly concealed substitute for feeding (see, for example, 1.9.10–11; 4.5.191–94, 222–24); and the unsatisfied ravenous attack of the infant on the breast provides the motive force for warfare. The image allows us to understand the ease with which Coriolanus turns his rage toward his own feeding mother, Rome.

Thrust prematurely from dependence on his mother, forced to feed himself on his own anger, Coriolanus refuses to acknowledge any neediness or dependency: for his entire sense of himself depends on his being able to see himself as a self-sufficient creature. The desperation behind his claim to self-sufficiency is revealed by his horror of praise, even the praise of his general: the dependence of his masculinity on warfare in fact makes praise (or flattery, as he calls it) particularly threatening to him on the battlefield; susceptibility to flattery there, in the place of the triumph of his independence, would imply that the soldier's steel has grown "soft as the parasite's silk" (1.9.45). The juxtaposition of soldier's steel and parasite's soft silk suggests both Coriolanus's dilemma and his solution to it: in order to avoid being the soft, dependent, feeding parasite, he has to maintain his rigidity as soldier's steel. And the same complex of ideas determines the rigidity that makes him so disastrous as a political figure. The language in which he imagines his alternatives as he contemptuously asks the people for their voices and later as he gives up his attempt to pacify them reveals the extent to which his unwillingness to ask for the people's approval, like his abhorrence of praise, depends on his attitude toward food: "Better it is to die, better to starve, / Than crave the hire which first we do deserve" (2.3.112–13); "Pent to linger / But with a grain a day, I would not buy / Their mercy at the price of one fair word" (3.3.89–91). Asking, craving, flattering with fair words are here not only preconditions but also equivalents of eating: to refuse to ask is to starve, but starvation is preferable to asking because asking, like eating, is an acknowledgment of one's weakness, one's dependence on the outside world. "The price is, to ask it kindly" (2.3.75): but that is the one price Coriolanus cannot pay. When he must face the prospect of revealing his dependence on the populace by asking for their favor, his whole delicately constructed masculine identity threatens to crumble: in order to ask, a harlot's spirit must possess him; his voice must become as small as the eunuch's or the virgin's minding babies; a beggar's tongue must make motion through his lips (3.2.111–18). Asking, then, would undo the process by which he was transformed from boy or woman to man on the battlefield. That he imagines this undoing as a kind of reverse voice change, from man to boy, suggests the extent to which his phallic aggressive pose is a defense against collapse into a dependent oral mode, when he had the voice of a small boy. And in fact, Coriolanus's own use of language constantly reiterates this defense. Flattery and asking are the linguistic equivalents of feeding (1.9.51–52): they are incorporative modes that acknowledge one's dependence. But Coriolanus spits out words, using them as weapons. His invective is in the mode of Hector's wound, aggressively spitting forth blood: it is an attempt to deny vulnerability by making the very area of vulnerability into the means of attack.

Coriolanus's abhorrence of praise and flattery, his horror lest the people think that he got his wounds to please them (2.2.147–50), his insistence that he be given the consulship in sign of what he is, not as a reward (1.9.26), his refusal to ask—all are attempts to claim that he is *sui generis*. His attitude finds its logical conclusion in his desperate cry as he sees his mother approaching him at the end:

> I'll never
> Be such a gosling to obey instinct, but stand
> As if a man were author of himself
> And knew no other kin.
>
> (5.3.34–37)

The gosling obeys instinct and acknowledges his kinship with mankind; but Coriolanus will attempt to stand alone. (Since Coriolanus's manhood depends exactly on this phallic standing alone, he is particularly susceptible to Aufidius's taunt of "boy" when he has been such a gosling to obey instinct.) The relationship between Coriolanus's aggressive pose and his attempts to claim that he is *sui generis* are most dramatically realized in the conquest of Corioli; it is here that Coriolanus most nearly realizes his fantasy of standing as if a man were author of himself. For the scene at Corioli represents a glorious transformation of oral nightmare ("to th' pot" [1.4.47] one of his soldiers says as he is swallowed up by the gates) into a phallic adventure that both assures and demonstrates his independence. The dramatic action itself presents the conquest of Corioli as an image of triumphant rebirth: after Coriolanus enters the gates of the city, he is proclaimed dead; one of his comrades delivers a eulogy firmly in the past tense ("Thou wast a soldier / Even to Cato's wish" [1.4.55–56]); then Coriolanus miraculously reemerges, covered with blood (1.6.22), and is given a new name. Furthermore, Coriolanus's own battlecry as he storms the gates sexualizes the scene: "Come on; / If you'll stand fast, we'll beat them to their wives" (1.4.40–41). For the assault on Corioli is both a rape and a rebirth: the underlying fantasy is that intercourse is a literal return to the womb, from which one is reborn, one's own author. The fantasy of self-authorship is complete when Coriolanus is given his new name, earned by his own actions.

But despite the boast implicit in his conquest of Corioli, Coriolanus has not in fact succeeded in separating himself from his mother; even the very role through which he claims independence was designed by her—as she never tires of pointing out ("My praises made thee first a soldier" [3.2.108]; "Thou art my warrior: / I holp to frame thee" [5.3.62–63]). In fact, Shakespeare underlines Volumnia's point by the placing of two central scenes. In 1.3, before we have seen Coriolanus himself as a soldier, we see Volumnia first *describe* her image of her son on the battlefield and then *enact* his role: "Methinks I see him stamp thus, and call thus: / 'Come on you cowards, you were got in fear / Though you were born in Rome'" (1.3.32–34). This marvelous moment not only suggests the ways in which Volumnia herself lives through her son; it also suggests the extent to which his role is her creation. For when we see him in the next scene, acting exactly as his mother had predicted, we are left with the impression that he is merely enacting her enactment of his role. That he is acting under her direction even in the role designed to insure his independence of her helps to explain both his bafflement when she suddenly starts to disapprove of the role that she has created ("I muse my mother / Does not approve me further" [3.2.7–8]), and his eventual capitulation to her demand that he shift roles, here and at the end of the play. When he finally agrees to take on the role of humble supplicant, he is sure that he will act badly (3.2.105–6) and that he will lose his manhood in the process (3.2.111–23). For his manhood is secure only when he can play the role that she has designed, and play it with her approval. He asks her, "Why did you wish me milder? Would you have me / False to my nature? Rather say I play / The man I am" (3.2.14–16). But "I play the man I am" cuts both ways: in his bafflement. Coriolanus would like to suggest that there is no distance between role and self, but in fact suggests that he plays at being himself. Given that Volumnia has created this dilemma, her answer is unnecessarily cruel—but telling: "You might have been enough the man you are, / With striving less to be so" (3.2.19–20). Volumnia is right: it is the intensity and rigidity of Coriolanus's commitment to his masculine role that makes us suspect the intensity of the fears that this role is designed to hide, especially from himself.

The fragility of the entire structure by which Coriolanus maintains his claim to self-sufficient manhood helps to account for the violence of his hatred of the plebeians. Coriolanus uses the crowd to bolster his own identity: he accuses them of being exactly what he wishes not to be. He does his best to distinguish himself from them by emphasizing his aloneness and their multitudinousness as the very grounds of their being. Throughout, he associates his manhood with his isolation, so that "Alone I did it" becomes a sufficient answer to Aufidius's charge that he is a boy; hence the very status of the plebeians as *crowd* reassures him that they are not men but dependent and unmanly things, merely children—a point of view that Menenius seems to confirm when he tells the tribunes, "Your abilities are too infant-like for doing much alone" (2.1.36–37). His most potent image of the crowd is as a common mouth (3.1.22, 155) disgustingly willing to exhibit its neediness. He enters the play identified by the plebeians as the person who is keeping them from eating (1.1.9–10); and indeed, one of his main complaints about the plebeians is that they say they are hungry (1.1.204–7). Coriolanus himself has been deprived of food, and he seems to find it outrageous that others should not be. His position here is like that of the older brother who has fought his way into manhood and who is now confronted by an apparently endless group of siblings—"my sworn brother the people" (2.3.95), he calls them—who still insist on being fed by mother Rome, and whose insistence on their dependency threatens the pose of self-sufficiency by which his equilibrium is perilously maintained. Indeed, the intensity of his portrayal of the crowd as a multitudinous mouth suggests not only the neediness that underlies his pose, but also the tenuousness of the pose itself: his insistent portrayal of the plebeians as an unmanly mouth, as feminine where they should be masculine, in effect as castrated, suggests that his hatred of the crowd conceals not only his own hunger but also his fears for his own masculinity. It is characteristic of Coriolanus's transformation of hunger into phallic aggression that the feared castration is imagined predominantly in oral terms: to be castrated here *is* to be a mouth, naked in one's dependency, perpetually hungry, perpetually demanding.

Coriolanus's absolute horror at the prospect of showing his wounds to win the consulship depends partly, I think, on the complex of ideas that stands behind his characterization of the crowd. In Plutarch, Coriolanus shows his wounds; in Shakespeare, the thought is intolerable to him and, despite many promises that he will, he never does. For his wounds would then become begging mouths (as they do in *Julius Caesar* [3.2.225–26]), and their display would reveal his kinship with the plebeians in several ways: by revealing that he has worked for hire as they have (that is, that he and his deeds are not *sui generis* after all); by revealing that he is vulnerable, as they are; and by revealing, through the persistent identification of wound and mouth, that he too has a mouth, that he is a feminized and dependent creature. Moreover, the exhibition of his wounds to the crowd is impossible for him partly because his identity is sustained by exhibitionism of another sort. The phallic exhibitionism of his life as a soldier has been designed to deny the possibility of just this kinship with the crowd; it has served to reassure him of his potency and his aggressive independence, and therefore to sustain him against fears of the collapse into the dependent mode of infancy. To exhibit the fruits of his soldiership not as the emblems of his self-sufficiency but as the emblems of his vulnerability and dependence, and to exhibit them precisely to those whose kinship with him he would most like to deny, would transform his chief means of defense into a proclamation of his weakness: it would threaten to undo the very structure by which he lives.

Behind Coriolanus's rage at the plebeians, then, stands the specter of his own hunger and his own fear of dependence. But this rage is properly directed toward his mother: and though it is deflected from her and toward the plebeians and Volscians for much of the play, it finally returns to its source after he has been exiled from Rome. For Rome and his mother are finally one: although in his loving farewell his family and friends are wholly distinguished from the beast with many heads, by the time he has returned to Rome they are no more than a poor grain or two that must be consumed in the general fire (5.1.27). (Even in his loving farewell we hear a note of resentment when he consoles his mother by telling her, "My hazards still have been your solace" [4.1.28].) And as he approaches Rome, we know that the destruction of his mother will not be merely incidental to the destruction of his city. For in exiling him, Rome reenacts the role of the mother who cast him out; the exile is a reliving of the crisis of dependency that Coriolanus has already undergone. Coriolanus initially meets this crisis with the claim that he himself is in control of the independence thrust upon him, a claim akin to the infant's fantasy of omnipotent control over the forces that in fact control him: "I banish you!" (3.3.123). He then attempts to insure himself of the reality of his omnipotence by wishing on his enemies exactly what he already knows to be true of them ("Let every feeble rumour shake your hearts! / . . . Have the power still / To banish your defenders" [3.3.125–28]): few curses have ever been so sure of instantaneous fulfillment. Having thus exercised his rage and assured himself of the magical power of his invective, Coriolanus finally makes his claim to true independence: "There is a world elsewhere!" (3.3.135). But he cannot sustain this independence, cannot simply separate himself from the world of Rome; the intensity of his identification with Rome and with his mother forces him to come back to destroy both, to make his claim to omnipotent independence a reality by destroying the home to which he is still attached, so that he can truly stand as if a man were author of himself. The return to Rome is an act of retaliation against the mother on whom he has been dependent, the mother who has cast him out; but it is at the same time an acting out of the child's fantasy of reversing the roles of parent and child, so that the life of the parent is in the hands of the omnipotent child. For Coriolanus can become author of himself only by first becoming author of his mother, as he attempts to do here: by becoming in effect a god, dispensing life and death (5.4.24–25), so that he can finally stand alone.

But Coriolanus can sustain neither his fantasy of self-authorship nor his attempt to realize a godlike omnipotent power. And the failure of both leaves him so unprotected, so utterly devoid of a sense of self that, for the first time in the play, he feels himself surrounded by dangers: for the capitulation of his independent selfhood before his mother's onslaught seems to him to require his death. Indeed, as he cries out to his mother, he embraces his intuition of his own death with a passivity thoroughly uncharacteristic of him:

> O my mother, mother! O!
> You have won a happy victory to Rome;

But for your son, believe it, O, believe it,
Most dangerously you have with him prevail'd,
If not most mortal to him. But let it come.

(5.3.185–89)

His attempt to ward off danger by pleading with Aufidius is strikingly half-hearted; and when he says, "Though I cannot make true wars, / I'll frame convenient peace" (5.3.190–91), we hear the tragic collapse of his personality. We of course know by this time that the self-sufficient and aggressive pose by which Coriolanus maintains his selfhood is as dangerous to him as its collapse, that Aufidius plans to kill him no matter what he does (4.7.24–26, 56–57). It is a mark of the extent to which external dangers are for Coriolanus merely a reflection of internal ones that he feels himself in no danger until the collapse of his defensive system. But Volumnia achieves this collapse partly because she makes the dangers inherent in his defensive system as terrifying as those which it is designed to keep at bay: her last confrontation with her son is so appallingly effective because she invalidates his defenses by threatening to enact his most central defensive fantasies, thereby making their consequences inescapable to him.

The very appearance of his mother, coming to beg him for the life of her city and hence for her own life, is an enactment of his attempt to become the author of his mother, his desire to have power over her. He has before found her begging intolerable (3.2.124–34); when she kneels to him here, making the role reversal of mother and child explicit (5.3.56), he reacts with an hysteria that suggests that the acting out of this forbidden wish threatens to dissolve the very structures by which he orders his life:

What's this?
Your knees to me? to your corrected son?
Then let the pebbles on the hungry beach
Fillip the stars. Then let the mutinous winds
Strike the proud cedars 'gainst the fiery sun,
Murd'ring impossibility, to make
What cannot be, slight work!

(5.3.56–62)

At first sight, this speech seems simply to register Coriolanus's horror at the threat to hierarchy implied by the kneeling of parent to child. But if Coriolanus were responding only—or even mainly—to this threat, we would expect the threatened chaos to be imaged as high bowing to low; and this is in fact the image that we are given when Volumnia first bows to her son as if—as Coriolanus says— "Olympus to a molehill should / In supplication nod" (5.3.30–31). But Coriolanus does not respond to his mother's kneeling with an image of high bowing to low; instead, he responds with two images of low mutinously striking at high. The chaos imaged here is not so much a derivative of his mother's kneeling as of the potential mutiny that her kneeling seems to imply: for her kneeling releases the possibility of his mutiny against her, a mutiny that he has been suppressing all along by his exaggerated deference to her. His response here reveals another of the bases for his hatred of the mutinous and leveling populace: the violence of his images suggests that his mother's kneeling has forced him to acknowledge his return to Rome as a rising up of the hungry and mutinous forces in himself. With her usual acumen, Volumnia recognizes the disarming of potential mutiny in Coriolanus's response and chooses exactly this moment to assert, once again, his dependence on her: "Thou art my warrior" (5.3.62).

The living out of Coriolanus's forbidden wish to have power over his mother had seemed to Coriolanus impossible; but now that protective impossibility itself seems murdered, and he is forced to confront the fact that his wish has become a reality. Nor are the hungry and mutinous forces within himself content to murder only an abstract "impossibility": the murderousness of the image is directed ultimately at his mother. And once again, Volumnia makes Coriolanus uncomfortably clear to himself: after she has enacted his terrifying fantasy by kneeling, she makes it impossible for him to believe that her death would be merely an incidental consequence of his plan to burn Rome. For she reveals exactly the extent to which he has identified mother and Rome, the extent to which his assault is on both. Her long speech builds to its revelation with magnificent force and logic. She first forces him to see his attack on his country as an attack on a living body by accusing him of coming to tear "his country's bowels out" (5.3.103). Next, she identifies that body as their common mother ("the country, our dear nurse" [5.3.110]). Finally, as she announces her intention to commit suicide, she makes absolute the identification of the country with herself; after she has imagined him treading on his country's ruin (5.3.116), she warns him:

> thou shalt no sooner
> March to assault thy country than to tread—
> Trust to't, thou shalt not—on thy mother's womb
> That brought thee to this world.
>
> (5.3.122–25)

The ruin on which Coriolanus will tread will be his mother's womb—a warning accompanied by yet another assertion of his dependence on her as she recalls to him the image of himself as a fetus within that womb.

If Coriolanus's mutinous fantasies are no longer an impossibility, if his mother will indeed die as a result of his actions, then Coriolanus will have realized his fantasy of living omnipotently without kin, without dependency. In fact this fantasy, his defense throughout, is articulated only here, as he catches sight of his mother (5.3.34–37); and its expression is the last stand of his claim to independence. Throughout this scene, Volumnia has simultaneously asserted his dependence on her and made the dangers inherent in his defense against that dependence horrifyingly clear; and in the end it is the combination of her insistence on his dependency and her threat to disown him, to literalize his fantasy of standing alone, that causes him to capitulate. Finally, he cannot "stand / As if a man were author of himself / And knew no other kin"; he must become a child again, a gosling, and admit his neediness. The presence of his own child, holding Volumnia's hand, strengthens her power over him: for Coriolanus seems to think of his child less as his son than as the embodiment of his own childhood and the child that remains within him; even when we are first told about the son, he seems more of a comment on Coriolanus's childhood than on his fatherhood. The identification of father and child is suggested by Coriolanus's response as he sees wife, mother, and child approaching: "My wife comes foremost; then the honour'd mould / Wherein this trunk was fram'd, and in her hand / The grandchild to her blood" (5.3.22–24). Here Coriolanus does not acknowledge the child as his and his wife's: he first imagines himself in his mother's womb, and then imagines his child as an extension of his mother. Even Coriolanus's language to Menenius as he earlier denies his family reveals the same fusion of father and son: "Wife, mother, child, I know not" (5.2.80) he says, in a phrase that suggests that his own mother is the mother of the child, and the child he attempts to deny is himself. Volumnia had once before brought Coriolanus to submission by reminding him of himself as a suckling child (3.2.129); now virtually her last words enforce his identification with the child that she holds by the hand: "This fellow had a Volscian to his mother; / His wife is in Corioles, and his child / Like him by chance" (5.3.178–80). But at the same time as she reminds him of his dependency, she disowns him by disclaiming her parenthood; she exacerbates his sense of himself as a child, and then threatens to leave him—as he thought he wished—alone. And as his fantasy of self-sufficiency threatens to become a reality, it becomes too frightening to sustain; just as his child entered the scene holding Volumnia's hand, so Coriolanus again becomes a child, holding his mother's hand.

The ending of this play leaves us with a sense of pain and anxiety; we are not even allowed the feelings of unremitting grief and satiation that console us in most of the other tragedies. The very nature of its hero insists that we keep our distance. Coriolanus is as isolated from us as he is from everyone else; we almost never know what he is thinking, and—even more intolerably—he does not seem to care what we are thinking. Unlike an Othello or an Antony, whose last moments are spent endearingly trying to insure our good opinion, Coriolanus makes virtually no attempt to affect our judgment of him: he dies as he has tried to live, heroically mantled in his self-sufficiency, alone. Nor is it only our democratic sympathies that put us uncomfortably in the position of the common people throughout much of the play: Coriolanus seems to find our love as irrelevant, as positively demeaning, as theirs; and in refusing to show the people his wounds, he is at the same time refusing to show them to us. In refusing to show himself to us, in considering us a many-headed multitude to whose applause he is wholly indifferent, Coriolanus denies us our proper role as spectators to his tragedy. The only spectators that Coriolanus allows himself to notice are the gods who look down on this unnatural scene and laugh, who are so far removed from men that they find this human tragedy a comedy. And as spectators we are in danger of becoming as distant from human concerns as the gods: for Coriolanus's isolation infects the whole play and ultimately infects us. There are very few moments of relaxation; there is no one here to love. We are made as rigid and cold as the hero by the lack of anything that absolutely commands our human sympathies, that demonstrates to us that *we* are dependent creatures, part of a community. Even the language does not open out toward us, nor does it create the sense of the merging of meanings, the melting together, that gives us a measure of release in *King Lear* or *Antony and Cleopatra,* where a world of linguistic fusion suggests the dependence of all parts. Instead, the language works to define and separate, to limit possibilities, almost as rigidly as Coriolanus himself does. And finally, the nature of our involvement in the fantasies embodied in this distant and rigid hero does not permit any resolution: it also separates and limits. For Coriolanus has throughout given free expression to *our* desire to be independent, and we delight in his claim. But when he turns on his mother in Rome, the consequences of his claim to self-sufficiency suddenly become intolerably threatening to us. We want him to acknowledge dependence, to become one of us; but at the same time we do not want to see him give in, because to do so is to force us to give up our own fantasy of omnipotence and independence. Hence at the final confrontation we are divided against ourselves and no solution is tolerable: neither the burning of Rome nor the capitulation and death of our claims to independence. Nor is the vision of human dependency that the play allows any compensation for the brutal failure of our desire to be self-sustaining. In *Lear* and *Antony and Cleopatra,* dependency is finally shown to be what makes us fully human: however much the characters have tried to deny it, it finally becomes their salvation, and ours, as we reach out to them. But dependency here brings no rewards, no love, no sharing with the audience; it brings only the total collapse of the self, the awful triumph of Volumnia, and Coriolanus's terribly painful cry: "O mother, mother! / What have you done?"

Shakespeare's Imitation of the World

A. D. Nuttall

Coriolanus shows us an older Rome [than the city of Julius Caesar], a city which has just become something more than a strangely warlike country town. Pope wrote that Shakespeare not only noticed the difference between Romans and English people but also saw the difference between different stages of Roman development. In *Coriolanus* the populace is only a little less contemptible than the mob in *Julius Caesar,* but at least it is interested in its political rights. Rome is firmly and consciously republican. The day of the autocrat has not yet come. The play even exhibits some awareness of economic factors. The populace in *Coriolanus* is not a Marxian proletariat of first-order producers, nor is Coriolanus himself an economic parasite. The city lives by military conquest; conquest produces tribute and the citizens are sustained by a gratuitous dole. In warfare it appears that they have been of little use (though one itches to step outside the data of the play and dispute this). Coriolanus, because he is a great killer, is in this society a great provider.

Coriolanus is at one and same time a sort of Titan and a baby. Modern critical accounts of him perhaps stress the second too much at the expense of the first. We should not forget that if any of us were to meet him on a battlefield the patronizing critical smile would be wiped away very quickly. As a warrior he is almost superhuman. But at the same time he is like a two-year-old in his tantrums, his stubbornness, his tendency to stamp or hide his face.

From *A New Mimesis: Shakespeare and the Representation of Reality.* © 1983 by A. D. Nuttall. Methuen, 1983.

And then there is his pride. Here, as usual, Shakespeare refuses to give the sentimentalist an easy ride. It would be nice to think that Coriolanus's contempt for the people is unmixed folly. Shakespeare keeps the situation uncomfortable by insinuating on the one hand that Coriolanus's pride has something pathological in it and on the other hand that the people are in fact much as he describes them. Strange world, where only the egomaniac speaks the truth!

In *Julius Caesar* we saw a fundamental problem of democracy broached; what happens when the people choose tyranny? In *Coriolanus* we have another, still more fundamental problem, one so uncomfortable that people prefer to set it aside as "ludicrously abstract": what happens when it can be predicted that the people, through vice or folly will choose corruptly? Is democracy right if the *demos* is bad? What does the good man do, placed in such a society? If you make liberty a terminal value of democracy (that is, if you believe that liberty is not only good because it promotes happiness but is also good in itself and moreover is the most important good of all) then you have no difficulty in answering this question. You will oppose Coriolanus. Perhaps older Americans will do this more confidently than other people. W. H. Auden wrote in an introduction to Henry James's *The American Scene* that many Americans have given up *Romanitas*. *Romanitas,* for Auden, means making virtue prior to freedom. People who give up *Romanitas* are people who would rather do wrong freely than do right under compulsion. It is interesting in view of the applicability of this conception to *Coriolanus* that Auden chose to express his idea with a word which literally means "Roman-ness."

Of course the Rome shown by Shakespeare is not a democracy but a republic. Nevertheless, there are moments in both *Julius Caesar* and *Coriolanus* when the political wishes of the people make themselves felt. In the tribunician elections of *Coriolanus* one has an actual specimen of rudimentary democratic machinery.

In 3.1 Coriolanus is therefore in an odd position. He is standing for election and he despises the electors. Falsehood is beneath him. His open electoral programme is therefore to strip the people of the very rights they exercise in electing him. It is almost a logical paradox, and equally close to being a joke. For if the people elect him, by their shrewdness they disprove his theory. Coriolanus would then be like Groucho Marx, who resigned from a golf club because it proved itself—through electing him—insufficiently exclusive. At this stage in Shakespeare's play I suppose most of the spectators have begun to feel that Coriolanus is a little mad. Yet a strand of moral integrity persists in him. He had said at the beginning of the play that he believed the populace to be in truth so cowardly and stupid that they could not even pursue their own interest:

> Your affections are
> As a sick man's appetite, who desires most that
> Which would increase his evil.
>
> (1.1.175–7)

By the beginning of act 3 Coriolanus's contempt for the people has reached such a pitch that he can scarcely be expected even to think about their interests. But, if he did, he would maintain his course. He plainly believes that it would be to the advantage of the people if those rights which they exercise with so little intelligence were taken from them. And the strangely pitiless dramatist, who has not a grain of compassion for the hunger of the starving in this play, inserts not a line to show that Coriolanus is wrong.

Can Coriolanus ask the people to sign away their privileges by electing him? He might answer that a populace capable of self-knowledge could and should do so. But, as we saw, a populace capable of self-knowledge would be utterly unlike this populace. Self-knowledge would in *its* case disclose intelligence and, given this intelligence, it would actually be wrong to sign away political rights. Coriolanus really is in a logical prison. There is, seemingly, a fundamental discrepancy between his warrior nature and the very institutions of a civil polity.

This brings us to the central pathos of Coriolanus's nature and the central tension of the play. Coriolanus has been made, by his overwhelming mother, Volumnia, into an instrument of war. We know roughly how it was done from the episode in 1.3, where we are told how Coriolanus's son, little Marcius, a miniature replica of his father, chased "a gilded butterfly," caught it and let it go over and over again until he fell in the chase and then seized the butterfly and "*mammocked*" it—that is, tore at it with his teeth (1.3.64). Volumnia greets the story with an indulgent, reminiscent smile: "One on's father's moods." Plainly, Coriolanus was rewarded with love for displays of aggression.

Notice how odd bits and pieces of *King Lear* are floating in this play. Shakespeare, who is full of recyclings, never merely repeats himself. In *King Lear* there are two especially powerful images. The first occurs in Gloucester's line:

> As flies to wanton boys are we to th' gods—
> They kill us for their sport.
>
> (4.1.37–38)

The second comes when Lear, restored to sanity after his ordeal in the storm, is reunited with Cordelia. He says to her,

> So we'll live,
> And pray, and sing, and tell old tales, and laugh
> At gilded butterflies.
>
> (5.3.11–13)

When he was writing *King Lear* Shakespeare had a vision compounded, one suspects, of memory and imagination. The memory was of cruel village boys tormenting insects. Imagination showed him gods who, while possessed of superhuman power, were morally identical with those remembered boys. In *Coriolanus,* which is about a hero-god who is himself like a violent child, the images naturally rose again in his mind—not only in the picture of little Marcius teasing and tearing the gilded butterfly but also later, when Coriolanus's army is described as coming on with no less confidence

> Than boys pursuing summer butterflies,
> Or butchers killing flies.
>
> (4.6.94–6)

Volumnia, then, has forged Coriolanus as an instrument of war. But then she encounters a problem. She needs an instrument to achieve her political ends within the city and she has built her son in a way which does not serve her purpose. It is like trying to saw with a sword. At a word he will hack and kill, but he is set to shy away from the very idea of compromise or conciliation. Yet his mother's power over him remains the strongest force in his life. In 3.2 Volumnia tries in vain to get Coriolanus to sue for office and only succeeds when she gives up rational persuasion and instead remarks— quite lightly—that she will be very pleased with him if he does it (3.2.109). At once he does what she wants.

I have said that Coriolanus's character is one of great pathos. The pathos lies in the fact that he has no inside. All he has was given him by his mother and confirmed in him in the physical stress of battle. What existentialists say is true of man in general is certainly true of Coriolanus in particular—namely, that in himself he is a kind of nothing and acquires what positive nature he possesses by adventitious role-adoption. It may be thought that in asserting this I go too far for sane historical scholarship—for everyone knows that in the sixteenth and seventeenth centuries men had a very strong and firm sense of the real nature of man, and his place in the great chain of being. But the Elizabethan world picture, as unified and frozen by scholars, is a retrospective historical myth. The existentialist idea that man's original nature lies in the negation of all essence is anticipated by Pico della Mirandola, in his *De hominis dignitate.* There the philosopher tells how God created the world, and framed it as a great ladder, blazing with light and colour, every rung loaded with being, all disposed in hierarchical splendour; and how God, having completed his immense cosmos, paused, and then resolved to make something quite different. And so he made man, a creature with no given nature at all, and unleashed this little darkness into his glittering creation, a flickering total freedom among all the splendid certainties, and bade it *take on* any nature it chose, be it God, beast or devil. The idea belongs clearly with that immensely influential body of thought known as Hermetism. If one must look for a single cosmology appropriate to Shakespeare surely this fits better than the bland system expounded by E. M. W. Tillyard? Certainly it was current in Shakespeare's time. John Donne wrote in a "Letter to a Lord" (1624) that, "to make myself believe that our life is something, I use in my thoughts to compare it to something; if it be like anything that is something" and lyrically explored the idea of a constitutive negation in his "Nocturnall upon St. Lucies Day." A similar way of speaking and thinking appears in Shakespeare's play, when Cominius says of Coriolanus,

> He was a kind of nothing, title-less,
> Till he had forg'd himself a name i' th' fire
> Of burning Rome.
>
> (5.1.13–15)

From being a kind of nothing he became—never a person, but rather a *thing,* insentient, an instrument, a machine. He is repeatedly spoken of in these terms. Cominius calls him "a thing of blood" (2.2.107). Coriolanus himself, in strange exultation, cries out to his men, "O, me alone! Make you a sword of me?" (1.6.76). Cominius later says of him,

> He leads them like a thing
> Made by some other deity than Nature.
>
> (4.6.91–92)

and Menenius calls him both "engine" and "thing" (5.4.20, 24).
There is something very sad in the way this artfully brutalized piece
of nothingness is at last brought to deny its own conditioning. In
5.3. Coriolanus has returned to destroy Rome and his mother goes
out to dissuade him, just once more, from his natural course. As he
sees her coming he says, feeling himself weakening,

> I'll never
> Be such a gosling to obey instinct, but stand
> As if a man were author of himself
> And knew no other kin.
>
> (5.3.34–37)

Here Coriolanus clutches at a Stoic attitude for the support it gives
to the isolated self. Yet the speech expresses a wish, not an achievement. Here, surely, was one who existed as a mere relation before he
existed substantially as himself; he is, timelessly, a son before he is
a man.

Again I have written in a freely transparent language, treating
the character of Coriolanus as a study in possible psychology. To
write and think in this way is to find oneself engaged in a dialogue
with a text which proves richly responsive. A rigorously formal approach might easily prevent a reader or spectator from noticing the
wholly remarkable sense Shakespeare displays of the possible form-
ative tyranny of the parent. This alone is sufficiently astonishing in a
pre-Freudian writer and yet it is certainly there, in the text. The curious and the historically sceptical can discover how Shakespeare
found hints of his conception in Plutarch. But *Coriolanus* like *Julius
Caesar* is at the same time a study of cultural change. This time, the
conception we have labelled "shame-culture" is a little closer than it
was with Brutus.

There is no contradiction in saying both that Coriolanus exem-
plifies a particular cultural pattern and that his personality was
formed for him by another individual, his mother. Volumnia made
her son according to a still available cultural model, that of the warrior. Coriolanus is therefore an artificial, but therefore especially
pure, specimen of the type. Certainly he has the entire courage, the

big language and perhaps the unreadiness for marriage (think of Othello) which Shakespeare seems to associate with the kind. Moreover, Shakespeare, in setting forth the growing civic institutions of Rome as existing in tension with the warlike mode is working with almost the same subject matter as a modern cultural historian. A. W. H. Adkins, for example, in his *Merit and Responsibility* traces the process by which what he calls "the co-operative values" gradually came to replace the "competitive values," as Greek society gradually settled into relatively stable city states. Terms like "temperate" came to carry more ethical weight than terms like "brave." The level of historical abstraction we find in Adkins's book seems quintessentially modern. But Shakespeare picked up from Plutarch the fact that the early Romans made much of *virtus* in its etymological sense, "manliness," "virile heroism." He chose to exhibit this virile courage in a civic context to which it is not suited. The audience can quite simply watch "the co-operative virtues" gathering power in the forum. Shakespeare shows with great clarity, first, how useful Coriolanus is to Rome in time of war and, second, how much happier the city is without him once peace has been attained. The second observation is emphasized in 4.6 where the citizens greet each other courteously and Sicinius says,

> This is a happier and more comely time
> Than when these fellows ran about the streets
> Crying confusion.
>
> (4.6.27–29)

It is perhaps impossible to say with precision to what extent the shame-culture of Coriolanus has assumed the introverted form given to it by Stoicism. It might be said that the true shame-culture figure rejoices above all in glory, in reputation, and that Coriolanus's refusal to court the people shows in him the egoistic withdrawal of the Stoic. But we must remember that when Coriolanus goes among the people he is with men who to him are little better than slaves. Even Homer's Achilles or Ajax, the purest examples we have of archaic shame-culture, would balk at seeking the favour of such base people. Certainly there should be no suggestion in production that Coriolanus is here displaying the "co-operative" virtue of modesty. Coriolanus wishes to hide his scars from the populace, not because he thinks them insignificant, but because he thinks them too glorious. He says,

> To brag unto them 'Thus I did, and thus!'
> Show them th'unaching scars which I should hide,
> As if I had received them for the hire
> Of their breath only!
>
> (2.2.144–48)

The people correctly identify his reluctance as springing from aristocratic pride.

It is true that when we see Coriolanus amid his fellow warriors, flushed with victory in 1.9, he keeps up a certain social opposition to praise and it must be conceded that this alone places him in a post-shame-culture period. But his resistance is shallow compared with his violent revulsion in Rome. Indeed, it is little more than a half-embarrassed shrugging of the shoulders:

> I will go wash;
> And when my face is fair you shall perceive
> Whether I blush or no. Howbeit, I thank you.
>
> (1.9.68–70)

The battle over, his energy drains from him and with aristocratic negligence he fails to recall the name of the poor man who sheltered him, the man for whom a little earlier he had pleaded with equally typical aristocratic magnanimity. Nietzsche, who is the father of all modern cultural historians of antiquity, would recognize at once both the largeness and the shallowness of Coriolanus's aristocratic spirit.

Coriolanus is never the theoretic, conscious Stoic that Brutus is in *Julius Caesar*. Yet there remains one pivotal moment in the play when he momentarily attains true Stoic grandeur. It comes at the end of 3.3, when the people turn on him and the tribune Brutus cries out that he should be banished as an enemy of the people. Coriolanus looks down at them and says, "I banish you" (3.3.125) and turns his broad back on them. The Senecan dicta are all there. The mind is its own place. The Stoic man is citizen of the world, and cannot be exiled. But at the same time we see something else, a red-faced child, stamping and crying through his tears 'I'll send *you* away!' Here intuitive cultural history intersects with intuitive psychology. The moment is powerfully mimetic, with a comprehensiveness and, at the same time, a particularity which will not easily be matched. It is also pure genius.

Coriolanus and Interpretations of Politics: "Who Does the Wolf Love?"

Stanley Cavell

Something that draws me to *Coriolanus* is its apparent disdain of questions I have previously asked of Shakespearean tragedy, taking tragedy as an epistemological problem, a refusal to know or to be known, an avoidance of acknowledgment, an expression (or imitation) of skepticism. Coriolanus's refusal to acknowledge his participation in finite human existence may seem so obviously the fact of the matter of his play that to note it seems merely to describe the play, not at all to interpret it. It may be, however, that this lack of theoretical grip itself proposes a moral, or offers a conclusion, namely that *Coriolanus* is not exactly to be understood as a tragedy, that its mystery—supposing one agrees to something like a mystery in its events—will be located only in locating its lack or missing of tragedy, hence its closeness to tragedy.

But systematically to pursue this possibility would require— from me—following out a sense that this play presents a particular interpretation of the problem of skepticism as such (skepticism directed toward our knowledge of the existence of others), in particular an interpretation that takes skepticism as a form of narcissism. This interpretation does not in itself come to me as a complete surprise since a book I published a few years ago—*The Claim of Reason*—begins with an interpretation of Wittgenstein's *Philosophical Investigations* which takes his move against the idea of a private

From *Themes Out of School: Effects and Causes.* © 1984 by Stanley Cavell. North Point Press, 1984.

language (an idea which arises in his struggle against skepticism) as a move against a kind of narcissism, a kind of denial of an existence shared with others; and my book ends with a reading of *Othello* as a depiction of the murderous lengths to which narcissism must go in order to maintain its picture of itself as skepticism, in order to maintain its stand of ignorance, its fear or avoidance of knowing, under the color of a claim to certainty. What surprised me more in *Coriolanus* was its understanding of narcissism as another face of incestuousness, and of this condition as one in which language breaks down under the sense of becoming incomprehensible, of the sense of oneself as having lost the power of expression, what I call in *The Claim of Reason* the terror of inexpressiveness; together with the thoroughness with which Narcissus's fate is mirrored in the figure of Coriolanus, a figure whose every act is, by that act, done to him so perfectly that the distinction between action and passion seems to lose its sense, a condition in which human existence becomes precarious, if perhaps transcendable. I mention these connections with the philosophical issue of skepticism not because I pursue them further in the essay to follow but only to attest my conviction that a work such as a play of Shakespeare's cannot contribute the help I want from it for the philosophical issues I mention, unless the play is granted the autonomy it is one's power to grant, which means, seen in its own terms. What does this mean? What is a play of Shakespeare's? I will try to say something about these questions.

Something else also draws me. The way I have been understanding the conflicts the play engenders keeps sending me back over paths of thought that I believe many critics have found to be depleted of interest, or conviction; three paths, or branches of paths, in particular: (1) those that look in a Shakespearean play for something like an idea of theater, as it were for the play's concept of itself; (2) those that sense Christian stirrings and murmurings under the surface of the words; and (3) even those paths of thought that anticipate something you might call the origins of tragedy in religious ritual. I am, I suppose, as drawn to critical paths that others find empty as some poets are to words that others find flat. But to say fully why one is drawn to a work, and its work of interpretation, can only be the goal of an interpretation; and the motive of an interpretation, like what one might call the intention of the work it seeks, exists fully only in its satisfaction.

I expect, initially, general agreement on two facts about *Coriolanus*. First, compared with other Shakespearean tragedies this one lacks what A. C. Bradley called "atmosphere" (in his British Academy Lecture on the play, the decade after his *Shakespearean Tragedy*). Its language, like its hero, keeps aloof from our attention, as withdrawn, austere, as its rage and its contempt permit. Second, the play is about the organization of the body politic and about how that body is fed, that is, sustained. I expect, further, that readers from opposed camps should be willing to see that the play lends itself equally, or anyway naturally, to psychological and to political readings: both perspectives are, for example, interested in who produces food and in how food is distributed and paid for. From a psychological perspective (in practice this has in recent years been psychoanalytic) the play directs us to an interest in the development of Coriolanus's character. From a political perspective the play directs us to an interest in whether the patricians or the plebeians are right in their conflict and in whether, granted that Coriolanus is unsuited for political leadership, it is his childishness or his very nobility that unsuits him.

In the critical discussions I have read so far, the psychoanalytic perspective has produced more interesting readings than the political. A political reading is apt to become fairly predictable once you know whose side the reader is taking, that of the patricians or that of the plebeians; and whose side the reader takes may come down to how he or she sees Menenius's fable of the organic state, the Fable of the Belly, and upon whom he or she places the blame for Coriolanus's banishment. If few will consider it realistic to suppose that Coriolanus would have made a good political leader, fewer will deny that in losing him the city has lost its greatest hero and that this loss is the expression of a time of crisis in the state. It is a time of famine in which the call for revolt is made moot by the threat and the fact of war and invasion, followed by a time in which victory in the war, and bitterness over its conduct, creates the call for counter-revolt by the state's defender and preserver. In such a period of crisis everyone and no one has good arguments, everyone and no one has right on their side. In Aufidius's great description of Coriolanus at the end of act 4 he summarizes as follows:

> So our virtues
> Lie in th'interpretation of the time;
>
> . . . .
> One fire drives out one fire; one nail, one nail;
> Rights by rights founder, strengths by strengths do fail.

One might say that just this division of fire and right is the tragedy, but would that description account for the particular turns of just these events, as distinct from the losses and ironies in any revolutionary situation? Even the most compelling political interpretation—in my experience this is given in Bertolt Brecht's discussion with members of his theater company of the opening scene of the play—seems to have little further to add, in the way of interpretation, once it makes clear that choosing the side of the plebeians is dramatically and textually viable. This is no small matter. It shows that Shakespeare's text—or what we think of as Shakespeare's humanity—leaves ample room for distinctions among the "clusters" of citizens, and it shows the weight of their common position in opposition to that of the patricians. And I take this in turn to show that the politics of the play is essentially the politics of a given production, so that we should not expect its political issues to be settled by an interpretation of what you might call "the text itself."

Exactly the power of Brecht's discussion can be said to be its success in getting us *not* to interpret, not, above all, to interpret food, but to stay with the opening fact of the play, the fact that the citizens of Rome are in revolt because there is a famine (and because of their interpretation of the famine). They and their families are starving and they believe (correctly, for all we know) that the patricians are hoarding grain. Not to interpret this means, in practical or theatrical terms, that we come to see that this cluster is of human beings, individual human beings, who work at particular trades and who live in particular places where specific people await news of the outcome of their dangerous course in taking up arms. This fact of their ordinary humanity is the most impressive fact that can be set against the patricians' scorn of them—a fact that ought not to be visible solely to a Marxist, a fact that shows up the language of the leaders as mysterious and evasive, as subject to what one may think of as the politics of interpretation.

Yet we also feel that the pervasive images of food and hunger, of cannibalism and of disgust, do mean something, that they call upon us for some lines of interpretation, and that the value of attending to this particular play is a function of the value to individual human beings of tracing these lines.

Psychoanalysts naturally have focused on the images of food and feeding that link Coriolanus and his mother. In a recent essay, " 'Anger's My Meat': Feeding, Dependency, and Aggression in *Cor-*

iolanus," Professor Janet Adelman has given so clear and fair an account of some two decades of psychoanalytic interpretations of food and feeding in the play, in the course of working out her further contributions, that I feel free to pick and choose the lines and moments bearing on this aspect of things that serve my somewhat different emphases.

Twice Volumnia invokes nursing. Early she says to Virgilia, rebuking her for worrying about her husband:

> The breasts of Hecuba
> When she did suckle Hector, looked not lovelier
> Than Hector's forehead when it spit forth blood
> At Grecian sword, contemning.
>
> (1.3.43–46)

And in her first intercession with her son:

> Do as thou list.
> Thy valiantness was mine, thou suck'st it from me,
> But owe thy pride thyself.
>
> (3.2.127–29)

Both invocations lead one to think what it is this son learned at his mother's breast, what it is he was fed with, particularly as we come to realize that both mother and son declare themselves to be starving. It is after Coriolanus's departure upon being banished, when Menenius asks Volumnia if she'll sup with him, that she comes out with

> Anger's my meat; I sup upon myself
> And so shall starve with feeding.
>
> (4.2.50–51)

As Coriolanus mocks and resists the ritual of asking for the people's voices, his being keeps revolting, one time as follows:

> Better it is to die, better to starve,
> Than crave the hire which first we do deserve.
>
> (2.3.118–19)

I say that mother and son, both of them, *are* starving, and I mean throughout, always, not just when they have occasion to say so. I take Volumnia's vision of supping upon herself not to be a picture simply of her local anger but of self-consuming anger as the presiding passion of her life—the primary thing, accordingly, she would have to teach her son, the thing he sucked from her, of course under the name of valiantness. If so, then if Volumnia and hence Coriolanus are taken to exemplify a Roman identification of virtue as valor, they should further be taken as identifying valor with an access to one's anger. It is "in anger, Juno-like," godlike, that Volumnia laments (4.2.52–53); and it is this anger that the Tribune Sicinius is remarking as, in trying to avoid being confronted by her, he says, "They say she's mad" (4.2.9). Along these lines, I emphasize Coriolanus's statement about deserving rather than craving not as

> Better it is to *die,* better to *starve,*
> Than crave

as if he is asserting the rightness of a particular choice for the future; but as

> *Better* it is to die, *better* to starve,
> Than crave

as if he is reaffirming or confessing his settled form of (inner) life. I expect that the former is the more usual way of emphasis, but I find it prejudicial.

Coriolanus and Volumnia are—I am taking it—starvers, hungerers. They manifest this condition as a name or a definition of the human, like being mortal. And they manifest this as a condition of insatiability (starving by feeding, feeding as deprivation). It is a condition sometimes described as the infiniteness of desire, imposing upon the finiteness of the body. But starving for Volumnia and her son suggests that this infiniteness is not the cause of human insatiability but is rather its effect. It is the effect not of an endless quantity, as though the self had, or is, endless reserves of desire; but of an endless structure, as though desire has a structure of endlessness. One picture of this structure is given by Narcissus for whom what is longed for is someone longing, who figures beauty as longing. Starving by feeding presents itself to Coriolanus as being consumed by hunger, and his words for hungering are desiring and craving. And what he incessantly hungers for is . . . not to hunger, not to desire, that is, not to be mortal. Take the scene of interview by the people:

CORIOLANUS: You know the cause, sir, of my standing here.
THIRD CITIZEN: We do, sir; tell us what hath brought you to't.

CORIOLANUS: Mine own desert.
SECOND CITIZEN: Your own desert?
CORIOLANUS: Ay, not mine own desire.
THIRD CITIZEN: How not your own desire?

(2.3.66–72)

If you desire to be desireless, is there something you desire? If so, how would you express it; that is, tell it; that is, ask for it? Coriolanus's answer to this paradox is to become perfectly deserving. Since to hunger is to want, to lack something, he hungers to lack nothing, to be complete, like a sword. My speculations here are an effort to do justice to one's sense of Coriolanus as responding not primarily to his situation with the plebeians, as if trapped by an uncontrollable disdain; but as responding primarily to his situation with himself, as befits a Narcissus, trapped first by an uncontrollable logic. While I will come to agree with Plutarch's early observation or diagnosis in his *Life of Caius Martius Coriolanus* that Coriolanus is "altogether unfit for any man's conversation," I am in effect taking this to mean not that he speaks in anger and contempt (anger and contempt are not unjustifiable) but that while under certain circumstances he can express satisfaction, he cannot express desire and to this extent cannot speak at all: the case is not that he will not ask for what he wants but rather that he can want nothing that he asks. His solution amounts, as both patricians and plebeians more or less note, to becoming a god. What god? We have to get to this.

Let us for the moment continue developing the paradox of hungering. To be consumed by hunger, to feed upon oneself, must present itself equally as being fed upon, being eaten up. (To feed means both to give and to take nourishment, as to suckle means both to give and to take the breast.) So the other fact of Coriolanus's and Volumnia's way of starving, of their hunger, is their sense of being cannibalized.

The idea of cannibalization runs throughout the play. It is epitomized in the title question I have given to these remarks: "Who does the wolf love?" Menenius asks this of the Tribunes of the people at the opening of act 2. One of them answers, with undeniable truth: "The lamb." And Menenius, ever the interpretative fabulist, answers: "Ay, to devour him, as the hungry plebeians would the noble Marcius." The other Tribune's answer—"He's a lamb, indeed, that baas like a bear"—does not unambiguously deny Menenius's interpretation. The shock of the interpretation is of course that it is from the beginning the people, not the patricians, and least of all Coriolanus, who are presented as lambs, anyway as food for patrician wolves. In Menenius's opening effort to talk the people out of revolt he declares that "The helms o'the state . . . care for you like fathers," to which the First Citizen replies "Care for us! . . . If the wars eat us not up, they will; and there is all the love they bear us." This fantasy is borne out when the general Cominius speaks of Coriolanus's coming to battle as to a feast (1.9.10). And the idea of the warrior Coriolanus feeding on a weaker species may be raised again in the battle at Corioli in his threat to any soldier who holds back, "I'll take him for a Volsce / And he shall feel mine edge," allowing the suggestion of his sword as a piece of cutlery. The idea of an ungovernable voraciousness is furthered by Volumnia's association of her son with his son's tearing apart a butterfly with his teeth. On the other hand, when Coriolanus offers himself to Aufidius at Antium he expresses his sense of having been devoured, with only the name Caius Marcius Coriolanus remaining, devoured by "the cruelty and envy of the people" (4.5.77–78). And Menenius, whose sense of justice is constricted, among other things by his fear of civil disorder, is accurate in his fears, in the consequences they prophesy for Rome, and he will repeat his vision of civil cannibalism:

> Now the good gods forbid
> That our renowned Rome, whose gratitude
> Towards her deserved children is enrolled
> In Jove's own book, like an unnatural dam
> Should now eat up her own.
>
> (3.1.288–92)

All readers of this aspect of the play will recognize in this description of Rome as potentially a cannibalistic mother an allusion to Volumnia; and the identification of Volumnia and Rome is enforced in other ways, not least by Volumnia herself when in the second and final intercession scene she says to her son:

> thou shalt no sooner
> March to assault thy country than to tread
> (Trust to't, thou shalt not) on thy mother's womb
> That brought thee to this world.
>
> (5.3.121–24)

It is very much to the point to notice that in Menenius's vision of Rome as an "unnatural dam" an identity is proposed between a mother eating her child and a mother eating herself: if Rome eats up all Romans there is no more Rome, for as one of the Tribunes asks, "What is the city but the people?" (3.1.198).

The paradox and reciprocity of hungering may be found registered in the question "Who does the wolf love?" If the question is asking for the object of the wolf's affection, the more nearly correct grammar would seem to be: "Whom does the wolf love?" But this correctness (call it a patrician correctness, a refinement in which the plebeians apparently do not see the good) would rule out taking the question also in its opposite direction, grammatically strict as it stands, namely as asking whose object of affection the wolf is. (Who does love the wolf?) The answer given directly, "The lamb," does not rule out either direction, but as the ensuing discussion demonstrates, the direction will be a function of what or who you take the lamb to be, hence what the wolf. Both directions, the active and the passive constructions of the play's focal verbs, are operative throughout the action. I have mentioned this explicitly in the cases of feeding and suckling. But it is, I find, true less conspicuously, but pertinently, in such an odd moment as this:

CORIOLANUS: Let them hang.
VOLUMNIA: Ay, and burn too.
(3.2.23–24)

One of the functions in providing Volumnia with this amplification here strikes me as suggesting her sense of the inevitable reflexiveness of action in their Rome: are hanging and burning actions done to someone, or something "they" are, or will be, doing?

The circle of cannibalism, of the eater eaten by what he or she eats, keeps being sketched out, from the first to the last. You might call this the identification of narcissism as cannibalism. From the first: at the end of Coriolanus's first long speech he says to the citizens:

You cry against the noble Senate, who
(Under the gods) keep you in awe, which else
Would feed on one another.
(1.1.187–89)

And at the last: Rome devouring itself is the idea covered in the obsessive images of Coriolanus burning Rome. It was A. C. Bradley again who at the end of his British Academy Lecture pointed up the sudden and relentless harping, principally after the banishment, on the image of fire, of Rome burning. Bradley makes nothing further of the point but it is worth noting, in view of the theme of starving and cannibalism, that fire in this play is imagined under the description of it as *consuming* what it burns.

You may say that burning as a form of revenge is Coriolanus's projection onto Rome of what he felt Rome was doing to him. This cannot be wrong, but it so far pictures Coriolanus, in his revenge, to be essentially a man like Aufidius, merely getting even; the picture requires refining. Suppose that, as I believe, in Coriolanus's famous sentence of farewell, "I banish you!" (3.3.123), he has already begun a process of consuming Rome, incorporating it, becoming it. Then when the general Cominius tried in vain to plead with him to save Rome, and found him to be "sitting in gold, his eye / Red as 'twould burn Rome" (5.1.63–64), he somewhat misunderstood what he saw. He took Coriolanus to be contemplating something in the future whereas Coriolanus's eye was red with the present flames of self-consuming. Consuming the literal Rome with literal fire would accordingly only have been an expression of that self-consuming. Thus would the city understand what it had done to itself. He will give it—horribly—what it deserves. Thus is the play of revenge further interpreted.

These various understandings of cannibalism all illustrate the ancient sentiment that man is wolf to man. (The Roman Plautus, to whom Shakespeare is famously indebted, is credited with being the earliest nameable framer of the sentiment. A pertinent modern instance occurs in Brecht's *Threepenny Opera*.) But the question "Who does the wolf love?" has two further reaches which we must eventually consider. First, there is the repetition of the idea that devouring can be an expression of love. Second, if, as I think, there is reason here to take the image of the wolf as the figure of the mythical animal identified with Rome, the one who suckled the founders of Rome (Volumnia is the reason), there is reason to take the lamb it is said to love (or that loves it) as the mythical animal identified with Christ.

Before this, I should make explicit a certain way in which the account of Coriolanus's motivation I have been driving at is somewhat at odds with the direction of psychoanalytic interpretation summarized and extended by Janet Adelman. She understands Coriolanus's attempt to make himself inhumanly independent as a defense against his horror of dependence, and his rage as converting his wish to be dependent against those who render him so. A characteristic turn of her argument consists of a reading of some lines I have already had occasion to quote [elsewhere]:

> The breasts of Hecuba
> When she did suckle Hector, look'd not lovelier
> Than Hector's forehead when it spit forth blood
> At Grecian sword, contemning.

Adelman reads as follows:

> Blood is more beautiful than milk, the wound than the breast, warfare than peaceful feeding. . . . Hector is transformed immediately from infantile feeding mouth to bleeding wound. For the unspoken mediator between breast and wound is the infant's mouth: in this imagistic transformation, to feed is to be wounded; the mouth becomes the wound, the breast the sword. . . . But at the same time as Volumnia's image suggests the vulnerability inherent in feeding, it also suggests a way to fend off the vulnerability. In her image, feeding, incorporating, is transformed into spitting out, an aggressive expelling; the wound once again becomes the mouth that spits. . . . The wound spitting blood thus becomes not a sign of vulnerability but an instrument of attack.

This is very fine and it must not be denied. But the transformation of Hector's mouth into a wound must not in turn deny two further features of these difficult lines. First, when Hector contemns Grecian swords, he is also to be thought of as fighting, as wielding a sword, so the mouth is transformed into, or seen as, a cutting weapon: the suckling mother is presented as being slashed by the son-hero, eaten by the one she feeds. Suffering such a fantasy would constitute some of Volumnia's more normal moments. Second, the lines set up an equation between a mother's milk and a man's blood, suggesting that we must understand the man's spitting blood in battle not simply as attacking but equally, somehow, as providing food, in a male fashion. But how? Remember that Coriolanus's way to avoid asking for something, that is, to avoid expressing desire, is by what he calls deserving the thing. His proof of desert is his valiantness, so his spitting blood in battle is his way of deserving being fed, that is to say, being devoured, being loved unconditionally. (War and feeding have consistently been joined in the words of this play. A Plebeian says: "If the wars eat us not up they will" (1.1.85–86). And Cominius: Coriolanus "cam'st to . . . this feast having fully dined before" (1.9.10–11); but again Cominius does not get the connection complete.) To be fed by Volumnia is to be fed *to* her. But since the right, or effective, bleeding depends (according to the equation of blood and milk) upon its being a form of feeding, of giving food, providing blood identifies him with his mother. His mother's fantasy here suggests that the appropriate reciprocation for having nourished her son is for him to become her, as if to remove the arbitrariness in her having been born a woman; and since it is a way of putting her into the world it is a way of giving birth to her. Her son's companion fantasy of reciprocation would be to return Rome's gift, to nurse Rome with the valiantness he sucked from it.

This fantasy produces contradictions which are a match for the fury of contradictions one feels in Coriolanus's position (for example, between the wishes for dependence and for independence). For he can only return his nourishment if Rome—taken as the people—deserves it. Hence the people's lack of desert entails his lack of desert, entails that he cannot do the thing that acquires love; he is logically debarred from reciprocating. The fact that he both has absolute contempt for the people and yet has an absolute need for them is part of what maddens him. (This implies again that I cannot understand Coriolanus's emotions toward the people as directed simply to, say, their cowardice, their being poor fighters. I am taking it that he needs their desert for, so to speak, private reasons as much as public.) The other part of what maddens him is that neither the people nor his mother—neither of the things that mean Rome—will understand his position. Neither understands that his understanding of his valiantness, his virtue, his worth, his deservingness, is of himself as a provider, and that this is the condition of his receiving his own sustenance. (This assumes that he shares his mother's fantasy of the equation of milk and blood—as if there is nothing in her he has not taken in.) The people, precisely on the contrary, maddeningly accuse him of *withholding* food; and his mother precisely regards his heroism purely as toughness, devoid of tenderness; or pure fatherhood devoid of motherhood; and as deserving something more than acknowledging what he provides, more than the delicate balance of his self-account, as if being made consul were indeed something more. ("Know, good mother, / I had rather be their servant in my

way / Than sway with them in theirs" [2.1.107–9].) In these mis-
understandings they have both already abandoned him, weaned him,
before the ritual of being made consul comes to grief and he is formally banished. This prior rejection, not just once but always, inherently, would allow the understanding of his anger as his mother
interprets anger, that is, as lamentation ("Anger's my meat . . . la-
ment as I do, / In anger, Juno-like"). We may not contradict her
interpretation, though we may interpret it further. We might go on
to interpret it as depression.

I might characterize my intention in spelling out what I call
these fantasies as an attempt to get at the origin of words, not the
origin of their meaning exactly but of their production, of the value
they have when and as they occur. I have characterized something
like this ambition of criticism variously over the years, and related it
to what I understand as the characteristic procedure of ordinary language philosophy. (One such effort enters into the opening pages of
"The Avoidance of Love: A Reading of *King Lear.*") And do my
spellings out help? Do they, for example, help comprehend Coriolanus's subsequent course—how he justifies his plan to burn Rome
and how he is talked out of his plan by his mother? It is not hard to
encourage oneself in the impression that one understands these
things. To me they seem mysteries. I will sketch the answers I have
to these questions and then conclude by indicating how these answers serve to interpret our relation to this play, which means to me,
to understand what a Shakespearean play is (as revealed in this
instance).

I pause, in turning to these questions, to make explicit an issue
that at any time may nag our consciousness of the play. The mother-
relation is so overwhelmingly present in this play that we may not
avoid wondering, at least wondering whether we are to wonder,
what happened to the father. The play seems to me to raise this question in three ways, which I list in decreasing order of obviousness.
First, Menenius is given a certain kind of fatherly role, or a role as a
certain kind of father, but the very difficulty of conceiving of him as
Coriolanus's real father, which is to say, as Volumnia's husband and
lover, keeps alive our imagination of what such a figure might look
like. Second, Coriolanus's erotic attachment to battle and to men
who battle suggests a search for the father as much as an escape from
the mother. This would afford an explanation for an otherwise, to
me, insufficiently explained use in the play of the incident from Plutarch's *Life* in which Coriolanus asks, exhausted from victorious

battle, that a man in the conquered city of Corioli be spared slavery on the ground that Coriolanus had "sometime lay at the poor man's house," a man whose name Coriolanus discovers he has forgotten. The vagueness of the man's identity and Coriolanus's expression of confusion in the Shakespeare—distinct differences from the occurrence of the incidents in Plutarch—suggest to my mind that the unnamed figure to whom Coriolanus wishes to provide reparation is, vaguely, transiently, an image of his father.

Third, and so little obvious as to be attributable to my powers of hallucination, Coriolanus's efforts at mythological identification as he sits enthroned and entranced before Rome is an effort—if one accepts one stratum of description I will presently give of him—to come unto the Father. (I will not go into the possibilities here, or fantasies, that a patrician matron is simultaneously father-mother, or that, in replacing his father, he becomes his own father.)

I was about to ask how we are to grasp Coriolanus's return and his change of heart. My answer depends on plotting a relation between him and the other sacrificial lamb I have mentioned, the lamb of God, Christ. I say plotting a relation between the figures, not at all wishing to identify them. I see Coriolanus not so much as imitating Christ as competing with him. These are necessarily shadowy matters and while everything depends on accuracy in defining this relation all I can do here is note some elements that will have to figure in the plotting.

Earlier I spoke of Coriolanus's solution to the paradox of hungering not to hunger, of wanting not to want, of asking not to ask, as one of becoming a god. Now we may see that Christ is the right god because of the way he understands his mission as providing non-literal food, food for the spirit, for immortality; and because it is in him that blood must be understood as food. If one is drawn to this as a possibility, one may find surprising confirmation for it in certain of Coriolanus's actions and in certain descriptions of his actions. (I am not interested in claiming that Coriolanus is *in some sense* a scapegoat, the way perhaps any tragic hero is; but in claiming that he is a specific inflection of *this* scapegoat.)

First his actions, two especially. First is his pivotal refusal to show his wounds. I associate this generally with the issue of Christ's showing his wounds to his disciples, in order to show them the Lord—that is, to prove the resurrection—and specifically with his saying to Thomas, who was not present at the first showing and who made seeing the wounds a condition of believing, that is, of declaring his faith, "Thomas, because thou hast seen me, thou believest: blessed are they that have not seen, and have believed" (John 20:29). (Thomas would not believe until he could, as he puts it and as Jesus will invite him to, "put mine hand into his side"; Aufidius declares the wish to "wash my fierce hand in's heart" (1.10.27.) I make no further claims on the basis of this conjunction; I can see that some good readers may feel that it is accidental. I do claim that good reading may be guided, or inspired, by the over-excitement such conjunctions can cause.) The second action is the second intercession, in which Volumnia, holding her son's son by the hand, together with Virgilia and Valeria appear to Coriolanus before Rome. I take this to invoke the appearance, while Christ is on the cross, of three women whose names begin with the same letter of the alphabet (I mean begin with M's, not with V's), accompanied by a male he loves, whom he views as his mother's son (John 19:25–27). (Giving his mother a son presages a mystic marriage.)

I do not suppose that one will be convinced by these relations unless one has antecedently felt some quality of—what shall I say?—the mythic in these moments. This is something I meant in calling these relations "shadowy matters": I meant this not negatively but positively. It is a way to understand Volumnia's advice to Coriolanus that when he makes his appeal to the people he act out the meaning of his presence:

> for in such business
> Action is eloquence, and the eyes of th'ignorant
> More learned than the ears.
>
> (3.2.75–77)

I accept this as advice Shakespeare is giving to his own audience, a certain hint about why the words of this particular play may strike one as uncharacteristically ineloquent.

The second source of confirmation for Coriolanus's connection with the figure of Christ lies, I said, in certain descriptions of his actions. I specify now only some parallels that come out of Revelation. In that book the central figure is a lamb (and there is also a dragon), and a figure who sits on a special horse and on a golden throne, whose name is known only to himself, whose "eyes were as a flame of fire," and who burns a city which is identified as a woman; it is, in particular, the city (Babylon) which in Christian tradition is identified with Rome. And I associate the opening of Coriolanus's opening diatribe against the citizens, in which he rebukes their wish for "good words" from him—glad tidings—accusing them of liking "neither peace nor war," with the message Christ dictates to the writer of Revelation: "I know thy works, that thou art neither cold nor hot; . . . Therefore, because thou art lukewarm, and neither cold nor hot, it will come to pass that I shall spew thee out of my mouth" (Rev. 3:15–16). (An associated text from Plutarch [North's translation] would be: "So Martius, being a stowte man of nature, that never yelded in any respect, as one thincking that to overcome all-wayes, and to have the upper hande in all matters, was a Token of magnanimities, and of no base and fainte corage, which spitteth out anger from the most weake and passioned parte of the harte, much like the matter of an impostume: went home." Whatever the ambiguities in these words, the general idea remains, indelibly, of Coriolanus's speech, when angry, as being the spitting forth of the matter of an abscess. This play about food is about revoltedness and disgust. *Coriolanus* and Revelation are about figures who are bitter, disgusted by those whom they have done good, whose lives they have sustained.) (Coriolanus's sense of disgust with the people is more explicitly conveyed by Shakespeare through the sense of their foul smell than of their foul taste. Shakespeare does use the idea of spitting twice: once, as cited, to describe Hector's forehead bleeding in battle, and the second time in Coriolanus's only scene of soliloquy, disguised before Aufidius's house: "Then know me not. Lest that thy wives with spits and boys with stones / In puny battle slay me"—so that both times spitting is linked with battle and with food. As I have implied, I understand Coriolanus's vision of his death in Antium at the hands of wives and boys as a prophecy of the death he actually undergoes there, spitted by the swords of strange boys.)

Conviction, or lack of it, in these relations is something one has naturally to assess for oneself. Granted that they are somehow at work, they work to make comprehensible what Coriolanus's identification with the god is (they are identified as banished providers of spiritual food) and what his justification for destruction is (the people lack faith and are to suffer judgment) and why he changes his mind about the destruction. It is, I think, generally felt that his mother prevails with him by producing human, family feeling in him, in effect showing him that he is not inhuman. This again cannot be wrong, but first of all he has his access of family feeling the moment he sees the four figures approaching (a feeling that does not serve to carry the day), and second, his feeling, so conceived, does not seem to me to account for Coriolanus's words of agony to his mother as he relents and "Holds her by the hand, silent."

> O mother, mother!
> What have you done? Behold, the heavens do ope,
> The gods look down, and this unnatural scene
> They laugh at. O my mother, mother! O!
> You have won a happy victory to Rome;
> But, for your son—believe it, O, believe it!—
> Most dangerously you have with him prevailed,
> If not most mortal to him. But let it come.
>
> (5.3.182–89)

(I say these are words of agony, but so far as I recall, no critic who cites them seems to find them so. I feel here especially at a disadvantage in never having been at a performance of *Coriolanus*. But I find on reading this passage, or rather in imagining it said (sometimes as by specific actors; Olivier, of course, among them, and the young Brando) that it takes a long time to get through. Partly that has to do with the fact of the repetition of words in the passage; partly with the specific words that are repeated, "O," "mother," and "believe it." It has further to do, I feel sure, with my uncertainty about how long the silences before and within this speech are to be held—a speech which may be understood as expressing the silence with which this son holds, and then relinquishes, his mother's hand. Suppose we try imagining that he does not relinquish her hand until just before the last sentence, "But let it come"—as if what is to come is exactly expressive of their separating, or say that of Rome from Rome. Then how far do we imagine that he goes through the imagining of what is to come, and how long would the imagining take, before he takes upon himself the words that invite its coming?) What it means that she may be "most mortal" to him cannot be that he may be killed— the mere fact of death is hardly what concerns this man. He must mean somehow that she has brought it about that he will have the wrong death, the wrong mortality, a fruitless death. Has she done this by showing him that he has feelings? But Christ, even by those who believe that he is the Lord, is generally held to have feelings. Coriolanus's speech expresses his agonized sense that his mother does not know who he is, together with an agonized plea for her belief. She has deprived him of heaven, of, in his fantasy, sitting beside his father, and deprived him by withholding her faith in him, for if she does not believe that he is a god then probably he is not a god, and certainly nothing like the Christian scenario can be fulfilled, in which a mother's belief is essential. If it were his father who sacrificed him for the city of man then he could be a god. But if it is his mother who sacrifices him he is not a god. The logic of his situation, as well as the psychology, is that he cannot sacrifice himself. He can provide spiritual food but he cannot make himself into food, he cannot say, for example, that his body is bread. His sacrifice will not be redemptive, hence one may say his tragedy is that he cannot achieve tragedy. He dies in a place irrelevant to his sacrifice, carved by many swords, by hands that can derive no special nourishment from him. It is too soon in the history of the Roman world for the sacrifice to which he aspires and from which he recoils.

And perhaps it is too late, as if the play is between worlds. I know I have been struck by an apparent incorporation in *Coriolanus* of elements from Euripides' *Bacchae,* without knowing how or whether a historical connection is thinkable. Particularly, it seems to me, I have been influenced in my descriptions by feeling under Coriolanus's final plea to his mother the plea of Pentheus to his mother, outside the city, to see that he is her son and not to tear him to pieces. The *Bacchae* is about admitting the new god to the city, present in one who is returning to his native city, a god who in company with Demeter's grain brings nourishment to mankind, one who demands recognition in order to vindicate at once his mother's honor and his being fathered by Zeus; the first in the city to acknowledge his divine descent are two old men. My idea is that Coriolanus incorporates both raging, implacable Dionysus and raging, inconstant Pentheus and that Volumnia partakes both of the chaste yet god-seduced Semele and of the mad and murderous Agave. Volumnia's identifying of herself with Juno (specifically, with Juno's anger) may thus suggest her sensing herself as the cause of her curse. It is not essential to my thought here that Shakespeare knew (of) Euripides' play. It is enough to consider that he knew Ovid's account of Pentheus's story and to suppose that he took the story as Euripides had, as about the kind of son (one unable to express desire) to whom the failure of his mother's recognition presents itself as a sense of being torn to pieces.

What is the good of such a tragedy of failed tragedy? Which is to ask: What is this play to us? How is it to do its work? This is the question I have been driving at and now that it is before us I can only state flatly, without much detail, my provisional conclusions on the topic.

They can by now be derived from certain considerations about Menenius's telling of the Fable of the Belly in the opening scene of the play. Every reader or participant has to make something of this extended, most prominently placed event. Until recent times most critics have assumed that Menenius is voicing a commonplace assumption of the times in which Shakespeare wrote and one that represents Shakespeare's view of the state—the state as a hierarchical organism, understandable on analogy with the healthy, functioning body. It is my impression that recent critics have tended not to dwell on the fable, as though the conservative way is the only way to take it and as though that vision is no longer acceptable, or presentable. But this seems to me to ignore what I take to be the three principal facts about Menenius's telling of the tale, the facts, one may say, of the drama in the telling. (1) The fable has competing interpretations. What the first citizen calls its "application" is a *question*. He and Menenius joke about whether the people or the patricians are better represented by the belly. (2) The fable is about food, about its distribution and circulation. (3) The fable is told (by a patrician) to citizens who are in the act of rising in revolt against a government they say is deliberately starving them, hence the patrician can be said to be giving them words *instead* of food. The first mystery of the play is that this seems to work, that the words stop the citizens, that they stop to listen, as though these citizens are themselves willing, under certain circumstances, to take words for food, to equate them.

Coriolanus's entrance at the end of the argument over the application of the fable confirms this equation of words and food: he has from the early lines of the play been identified as the people's chief enemy, here in particular as chief of those who withhold food; and his opening main speech to them, after expressing his disgust by them, is to affirm that he does withhold and will go on withholding "good words" from them. Accordingly every word he speaks will mean the withholding of good words. He will, as it were, have a sword in his mouth. There are other suggestions of the equation of words and food in the play (for example, the enlivening of the familiar idea that understanding is a matter of digesting) but this is enough for me, in view of my previous suggestions, to take the equation as part of the invocation of the major figure of our civilization for whom words are food. The word made flesh is to be eaten, since this is the living bread. Moreover, the parables of Jesus are characteristically about food, and are always meant as food. The words/food equation suggests that we should look again at Volumnia's intercession speeches, less for their content than for the plain fact of their drama, that they are much the longest speeches Coriolanus listens to, that they cause his mother to show him her undivided attention and him to give her his silence; he is as if filled up by her words. It pleases me further to remember that Revelation also contains a vision of words that are eaten: there is a book the writer swallows that tastes as sweet as honey in the mouth but bitter in the belly (10:10), as if beauty were the beginning of terror, as in, for example, a play of Shakespeare's.

My conclusion about the working of the play, about what kind of play it is, adds up then as follows. I take the telling of the Fable of the Belly as a sort of play-within-the-play, a demonstration of what Shakespeare takes his play—named for Coriolanus—to be, for *Coriolanus* too is a tale about food, with competing interpretations requiring application, told by one man to a cluster, call this an audience, causing them to halt momentarily, to turn aside from their more practical or pressing concerns in order to listen. Here is the relevance I see in the fact that the play is written in a time of corn shortages and insurrections. The fact participates not just in the imagery of the play's setting, but in the question of the authority and the virtue of portraying such a time, at such a time, for one's fellow citizens; a question of the authority and the virtue in being a writer. I see in Shakespeare's portrayal of the Fable of the Belly a competition (in idea, perhaps in fact) with Sir Philip Sidney's familiar citing of the fable in his *Defence of Poetry,* or a rebuke of it. Sidney records Menenius's application of the tale as having "wrought such effect in the people, as I never read that only words brought forth but then, so sudden and so good an alteration; for upon reasonable conditions a perfect reconcilement ensued." But in casting his partisan, limited Menenius as the teller of the tale, and placing its telling at the opening of the play, where we have minimal information or experience for judging its events, Shakespeare puts into question both the nature of the "alteration" and the "perfection" of the reconciliation. Since these are the two chief elements of Sidney's defense of poetry, this defense is as such put into question; but hence, since Shakespeare is nevertheless giving his own version of the telling of the fable, making his own story about the circulation of food, he can be understood as presenting in this play his own defense of poetry (more particularly, of plays, which Sidney particularly attacks). It is in this light noteworthy that Sidney finds "Heroical" poetry to be most "[daunting to] all back-biters," who would "speak evil" of writing which presents "champions . . . who doth not only teach and move to a truth, but teacheth and moveth to the most high and excellent truth." But since "the image of such worthies" as presented in such works "most inflameth the mind with desire to be worthy," and since *Coriolanus* is a play that studies the evil in such an inflammation, Shakespeare's play precisely questions the ground of Sidney's claim that "the Heroical . . . is not only a kind, but the best and most accomplished kind of Poetry."

What would this play's defense of poetry be, I mean how does it direct us to consider the question? Its incorporation of the Fable of the Belly I understand to identify us, the audience, as starvers, and to identify the words of the play as food, for our incorporation. Then we have to ask of ourselves, as we have to ask of the citizens: Why have we stopped to listen? That is, what does it mean to be a member of this audience? Do we feel that these words have the power of redemption for us?

They are part of an enactment of a play of sacrifice; as it happens, of a failed sacrifice. And a feast-sacrifice, whether in Christian, pre-Christian, Nietzschean, or Freudian terms, is a matter of the founding and the preserving of a community. A community is thus identified as those who partake of the same body, of a common victim. This strikes Coriolanus as our being caught in a circle of mutual partaking, incorporating one another. And this is symbolized, or instanced, by speaking the same language. A pervasive reason Coriolanus spits out words is exactly that they *are* words, that they exist only in a language, and that a language is metaphysically something shared, so that speaking is taking and giving in your mouth the very matter others are giving and taking in theirs.

It is maddeningly irrelevant to Coriolanus which party the belly represents. What matters to him is that, whoever rules, all are members, that all participate in the same circulation, the same system of exchange, call it Rome; that to provide civil nourishment you must allow yourself to be partaken of. This is not a play about politics, if this means about political authority or conflict, say about questions of legitimate succession or divided loyalties. It is about the formation of the political, the founding of the city, about what it is that makes a rational animal fit for conversation, for civility. This play seems to think of this creation of the political, call it the public, as the overcoming of narcissism, incestuousness, and cannibalism; as if it perceives an identity among these relations.

In constructing and contesting with a hero for whom the circulation of language is an expression of cannibalism, *Coriolanus* takes cannibalism as symbolic of the most human of activities, the most distinctive, or distinguished, of human activities. (Sidney cites the familiar conjunction: "Oratio, next to Ratio, . . . [is] the greatest gift bestowed upon mortality.") Coriolanus wishes to speak, to use words, to communicate, without exchanging words; without, let us say, reasoning (with others); to speak without conversing, without partaking in conversation. Here is the conversation for which he is unfit, call it civil speech. Hence I conceive *Coriolanus* to be incorporating Montaigne's interpretation of literal cannibalism as more civilized than our more sophisticated—above all, more pervasive—manners of psychological torture, our consuming others alive. (Finding the words/food representation so compelling, I am ignoring here the path along which the circulation of words also registers the circulation of money [as in "So shall my lungs/Coin words" (3.1.77–78); and in "The price is, to ask it kindly" (2.3.77)]. The sense of consuming as expending would relate to Coriolanus's frantic efforts to deny that his actions can be recompensed ["better to starve than crave the hire"—for example, of receiving voices *in return*]. Money depends upon the equating of values; Coriolanus on their lack of equation, on measurelessness, pricelessness.) Montaigne's "On Cannibals" is more specifically pertinent to this play: its story of a cannibal prisoner of a cannibal society valorously taunting his captors by reminding them that in previous battles, when he had been victorious over them, he had captured and eaten their ancestors, so that in eating him they will be consuming their own flesh—this is virtually the mode in which Coriolanus addresses himself to the Volscians in putting himself at their mercy. And more variously pertinent: the essay interprets cannibalism as revenge; and it claims (in one of those moods of measured hilarity) that when three men from a cannibal society visited Rouen and were asked what they found most amazing about the ways of Montaigne's countrymen, one of their responses was as follows (I will not comment on it but quote in Frame's translation):

Second (they have a way in their language of speaking of men as halves of one another), they had noticed that there were among us men full and gorged with all sorts of good things, and that their other halves were beggars at their doors, emaciated with hunger and poverty; and they thought it strange that these needy halves could endure such an injustice, and did not take the others by the throat, or set fire to their houses.

Within the experience of such a vision of the circulation of language a question, not readily formulatable, may press for expression: To what extent can Coriolanus (and the play that creates him and contests with him) be understood as seeing his salvation in silence? The theme of silence haunts the play. For example, one of Coriolanus's perfectly cursed tasks is to ask for "voices" (votes) that he exactly wishes not to hear. Again, the words "silent" and "silence" are beautifully and mysteriously associated, once each, with the women in his life: with his wife ("My gracious silence, hail!"); and with his mother ("He holds her by the hand, silent"). Toward both, the word of silence is the expression of intimacy and identification; but in his wife's case it means acknowledgment, freedom from words, but in a life beyond the social, while in his mother's case it means avoidance, denial, death, that there is no life beyond the social. The ambiguities here are drilled through the action of the play by the repeated calls "Peace, peace"—hysterical, ineffective shouts of this particular word for silence. The play literalizes this conventional call for silence by implying that speech is war, as if this is the reason that both words and war can serve as food. But the man for war cannot find peace in peace—not merely because he, personally, cannot keep a civil tongue in his head, but because a tongue is inherently uncivil (if not, one hopes, inveterately so). Silence is not the absence of language; there is no such absence for human beings; in this respect, there is no world elsewhere.

Coriolanus cannot imagine, or cannot accept, that there is a way to partake of one another, incorporate one another, that is necessary to the formation rather than to the extinction of a community. (As he cannot imagine being fed without being deserving. This is his precise reversal of Christ's vision, that we cannot in ourselves deserve sustenance, and that it is for that reason, and in that spirit, that we have to ask for it. Thus is misanthropy, like philanthropy, a certain parody of Christianity.) The play *Coriolanus* asks us to try to imagine it, imagine a beneficial, mutual consumption, arguing in effect that this is what the formation of an audience is. (As if *vorare* were next to *orare*).

It seems to me that what I have been saying demonstrates, no doubt somewhat comically, the hypothesis of the origin of tragedy in religious ritual—somewhat comically, because I must seem rather to have deflated the problem, implying that whether the hypothesis is true depends on what is meant by "tragedy," what by "origin," and which ritual is in mind. I have, in effect, argued that if you accept the words as food, and you accept the central figure as invoking the central figure of the Eucharist, then you may accept a formulation to the effect (not that the play is the ritual of the Eucharist, but to the effect) that the play celebrates, or aspires to, the same fact as the ritual does, say the condition of community. Eucharist means gratitude, precisely what Coriolanus feels the people withhold from him. This is another way to see why I am not satisfied to say that Coriolanus is enraged first of all by the people's cowardice. Perhaps one may say that to Coriolanus their cowardice means ingratitude. As for the idea of origin, we need only appeal to Descartes's idea that the origin of a thing is the same thing that preserves it. What preserves a tragedy, what creates the effect of a certain kind of drama, is the appropriation by an audience of this effect, our mutual incorporation of its words. When the sharing of a sacrifice is held on religious ground, the ritual itself assures its effectiveness. When it is shifted to aesthetic ground, in a theater, there is no such preexisting assurance; the work of art has to handle everything itself. You might think of this as the rebirth of religion from the spirit of tragedy. A performance is nothing without our participation in an audience; and this participation is up to each of us.

To enforce the necessity of this decision to participate (a decision which of course has its analogue for the individual reader with the script in his or her hands) is the way I understand the starkness of the words of this play, their relative ineloquence, their lack of apparent resonance. The play presents us with our need for one another's words by presenting withholding words, words that do not meet us halfway. It presents us with a famine of words. This way of seeing it takes it to fulfill a prophecy from the book of Amos 8:12: "Behold, the days come, saith the Lord God, that I will send a famine in the land, not a famine of bread, nor a thirst for water; but of hearing the words of the Lord."

Livy, Machiavelli,
and Shakespeare's *Coriolanus*

Anne Barton

In book 7 of his great history of Rome, from her foundation to the time of Augustus, Titus Livius recounts, with a certain admixture of scepticism, the story of Marcus Curtius. In the year 362 B.C. a chasm suddenly opened in the middle of the Forum. The soothsayers, when consulted, declared that only a ritual sacrifice of the thing "wherein the most puissance and greatness of the people of Rome consisted" could close the fissure and "make the state of Rome to remain sure forever." Much discussion followed, but no one could determine what that precious thing might be. Then Marcus Curtius, described in Philemon Holland's Elizabethan translation of Livy as "a right hardie knight and martiall yong gentleman," "rebuked them therefore, because they doubted whether the Romanes had any earthly thing better than armour and valor." Armed at all points, he mounted a horse "as richly trapped and set out as possible he could devise," and—like Hotspur at Shrewsbury—"leapt into destruction" (*2 Henry IV*, 1.3.33). The gulf closed.

In the Rome of Marcus Curtius, a century after the time of Coriolanus, it is by no means obvious that valour is "the chiefest virtue," the one to which the city still owes her greatness. Times have changed. The Romans need to be reminded, by the gods and by the heroic action of one "martiall yong gentleman," that formerly, as Plutarch asserts in his "Life of Coriolanus," "valliantnes was hon-

From *Shakespeare Survey: An Annual Survey of Shakespearian Study and Production* (Volume 38), edited by Stanley Wells. © 1985 by Cambridge University Press.

oured in Rome above all other vertues: which they called *Virtus,* by the name of vertue selfe, as including in the generall name, all other speciall vertues besides. So that *Virtus* in the Latin, was asmuche as valliantnes." This passage, in North's translation, caught Shakespeare's eye. But the version of it that he introduced into act 2, scene 2 of *Coriolanus* is qualified and uncertain. "It is held," Cominius says as he begins his formal oration in the Capitol in praise of Coriolanus,

> That valour is the chiefest virtue and
> Most dignifies the haver: if it be,
> The man I speak of cannot in the world
> Be singly counter-pois'd.
>
> (2.2.83–87)

"If," as Touchstone points out in *As You Like It,* is a word with curious properties and powers: "Your If is the only peacemaker; much virtue in If" (5.4.102–3). Cominius's "If," like Touchstone's, is a kind of peacemaker. Set off by the cautious appeal to an opinion in "it is held," it introduces a slight but significant tremor of doubt into what in Plutarch had been fact, rock-hard and incontrovertible. Cominius goes on to celebrate Coriolanus in battle as a huge, irresistible force—a ship in full sail, bearing down and cleaving the aquatic vegetation of the shallows, a planet, the sea itself—but "If" continues to mediate between martial prowess as a traditional all-sufficing good and the possible claims of other human ideals. It is as though Shakespeare's Cominius already had an intimation of that later Rome in which Marcus Curtius would be obliged to demonstrate to a forgetful city that valour was indeed her "chiefest virtue."

In writing *Coriolanus,* Shakespeare depended primarily upon Plutarch, as he had for *Julius Caesar* and *Antony and Cleopatra.* Once again, North's translation provided him with the dramatic skeleton, and even some of the actual words, of his play. But this time, he also had recourse to Livy, the chronicler of Coriolanus, Marcus Curtius, and the fortunes of republican Rome. It has long been recognized that lines 134 to 139 in Menenius's fable of the belly, those concerned with the distribution of nourishment through the blood, derive from Livy's, not Plutarch's, version of the tale. Those six lines are important in that they provide tangible evidence that Livy's *Ab Urbe Condita* was in Shakespeare's mind when he was meditating *Coriolanus.* But they matter far less than a series of overall attitudes, attitudes peculiar to this play, which I believe Shakespeare owed not to any one particular passage in Livy, but to his history as a whole—in it-self, and also as it had been interpreted by another, celebrated Renaissance reader.

As an author, Livy is likely to have impinged upon Shakespeare's consciousness at a relatively early age. Selections from his work were often read in the upper forms of Elizabethan grammar schools, ranking in popularity only behind Sallust and Caesar. As a young man, Shakespeare drew material from book 1 in composing his "graver labour," *The Rape of Lucrece,* published in 1594, six years before Philemon Holland's translation made the whole of Livy available in English. Shakespeare customarily consulted more than one historical source. He had never, before *Coriolanus,* written a play set in republican Rome, in a mixed state of the kind that, for various reasons, was attracting considerable attention in Jacobean England. Livy was the acknowledged, great repository of information about this republic, as well as its fervent champion. It was almost inevitable that Shakespeare should return to *Ab Urbe Condita,* now handsomely "Englished" by Holland, in order to remind himself of what was happening in Rome at the beginning of the fifth century B.C. What he found there was an account of Caius Martius which, although the same in its essentials as that of Plutarch in his "Life of Coriolanus," was different in emphasis, and radically altered by a context from which it could not be disentangled.

Unlike Plutarch, the biographer of great men, author of *Lives* carefully paired for moral and didactic purposes, Livy was preeminently the historian of a city. Throughout the thirty-five extant books of his history, he never breaks faith with the intention expressed in his very first sentence: to record the *res populi Romani,* the achievements of the people of Rome. By *"populi,"* Livy does not just mean plebeians. He means everyone, all classes, the rulers and the ruled, the leaders and the led. In Livy's eyes, no man, no matter how great, should regard himself as superior to the state, or even coequal. Plutarch consistently plays down the political concerns of Dionysius of Halicarnassus, one of his main sources of information as to the nature of Rome's past. Livy, by contrast, is far less interested in individual destiny than he is in the changing character of Rome's institutions, her expansion through the Mediterranean, and the increasingly complex social and economic equilibrium worked out within the city over a long period of time. So, characteristically, he does not find it especially important to determine whether Coriolanus himself was, in fact, killed by his Volscian allies after he turned back from the gates of Rome, or whether he survived, eating the bitter bread of exile, into old age. Either ending is possible. What really matters to Livy in the Coriolanus story is, first, that thanks to the intervention of the women, Rome herself escaped destruction and even acquired a fine new temple dedicated to Fortuna Muliebris. Secondly, that a new stage was reached in the protracted but necessary struggle between patricians and plebeians—a struggle in which there was right on both sides.

Although Collingwood perversely tried to deny it, Livy is essentially a developmental historian. As T. J. Luce writes in his recent study of the composition of Livy's history, "the central theme of his narrative is that the growth of Rome and the genesis of her institutions was a gradual, piecemeal process that took many centuries." Book 2, in which the story of Caius Martius is told, addresses itself specifically to the question of how *libertas* was achieved, actually, and in men's minds. It begins with threats from without: Lars Porsinna of Clusium and the attempt of the exiled Tarquins to regain control of the city. It ends with the overcoming of threats from within, represented by Spurius Cassius, and by Coriolanus. In describing the arrogance of Coriolanus, his stubborn refusal to countenance the tribunate, Livy writes with the Tarquin kings and their tyranny in mind, and also in full awareness of what (historically) was to come: an increase in the number of tribunes to ten, publication of the laws, permission for plebeian/patrician intermarriage, and the opening of the highest civic offices, including the consulship itself, to plebeians. Livy himself went on to chronicle these changes, leaving Coriolanus almost entirely forgotten in the past, except as the focus (intermittently remembered) of a cautionary tale. However useful in time of war, men like Coriolanus are a threat to the balance of the state, to an evolving republic which must try to take them with it but, if it cannot, has no option but to discard them by the way.

Although the populace in *Julius Caesar* includes one witty shoemaker, and there are—temporarily—two sceptics among the followers of Jack Cade, it would be hard to claim that Shakespeare displays much sympathy for urban crowds in the plays he wrote before *Coriolanus*. In depicting the fickle and destructive mob roused so skilfully by Mark Antony, the ignorant and brutal rebels of *2 Henry VI,* even those xenophobic Londoners rioting over food prices in the scene he contributed to *Sir Thomas More,* he is savagely funny, but also almost wholly denigratory. That is no reason for assuming, as critics tend to do, that his attitude in *Coriolanus* must be similar. In fact, this play is unique in the canon for the tolerance and respect it accords an urban citizenry. The very first scene of the tragedy presents plebeians who arrest their own armed rebellion in mid-course, not because of outside intervention by a social superior—the persuasive tactics of a Flavius and Marullus, a Lord Clifford or a Sir Thomas More—but freely, of their own volition, because it is important to them to inquire exactly what they are doing, and why. The Roman people here are not distinguished by personal names. They speak, nonetheless, as individuals, not as a mob. They care about motivation, their own and that of their oppressors, and they are by no means imperceptive. Even the belligerent First Citizen thinks it important to establish that hunger has forced him into violence, not a "thirst for revenge" (1.1.24). Not one of the citizens attempts to deny that Caius Martius has served Rome nobly, whatever his attitude towards them, nor do they make the mistake of thinking that he stands out against a distribution of surplus corn to the commons because he is personally covetous. The First Citizen contents himself with suggesting that this man's valorous deeds have been performed for suspect reasons: out of pride, and a desire to please his mother, rather than from disinterested love of his country. This is not very far from the truth. The Second Citizen has already cautioned the First against speaking "maliciously" (l. 34), and yet the events of the play will, to a large extent, justify the latter's analysis.

The Roman people in this play are politically unsophisticated and, sometimes, confused and naive. Like Williams and Bates confronting the disguised Henry V on the eve of Agincourt, they can be blinded by rhetoric, even though theirs is in fact the stronger case. The English common soldiers allowed themselves to be diverted from the crucial issue of whether or not Henry's cause in France was "good." The citizens of Rome are so impressed by the fable of the belly that they fail to detect the logical flaw in its application: the fact that in the present famine the senators are indeed selfishly "cupboarding the viand" (1.1.99) of last year's harvest in their storehouses, that the belly, by withholding nourishment from the rest of the body politic, has ceased to perform its proper social function. They also allow themselves to be manipulated by their tribunes. And yet it matters that, unlike the crowd in *Julius Caesar,* a crowd which has no opinions of its own, merely those which are suggested to it, first by Brutus and then by Mark Antony, the citizens of the republic can think for themselves. They draw their own conclusions, quite unaided, about the behaviour of Coriolanus when he stands in the marketplace and insultingly demands their voices. If, as the First Citizen says in that scene, the price of the consulship is "to ask it kindly" (2.3.75), Coriolanus at the end of it has been given something for nothing. The people sense this, although even here a dissenting voice is raised: "No, 'tis his kind of speech; he did not mock us" (2.3.159). "Almost all" the citizens, we are told—not all, because there are other, independent opinions—"repent in their election" (ll. 252–53). The tribunes deliberately inflame the commons against Coriolanus, finally transforming them from angry but rational individuals into "a rabble of Plebeians" (3.1.178). They are right, however, when they claim that they have a mandate from the people, that the sudden reaction against Coriolanus is "partly . . . their own" (2.3.260).

The worst thing the plebeians ever do is something for which Coriolanus himself never berates them. He is not present in Rome to witness their panic-stricken reaction to the news of his league with Aufidius, or the irrational fury they unleash upon Junius Brutus, their own tribune. This is almost the only occasion on which their behaviour can be said to approximate to that of Shakespeare's earlier crowds. In this play, it is exceptional rather than characteristic. It is true that, when cunningly prompted to do so by the tribunes in act 3, the plebeians claim that they alone embody Rome: "the people," they shout, "are the city" (3.1.198). This is patently false, as they themselves know in their calmer moods. Rome cannot be identified solely with her commons. But then, the assumption with which Menenius begins the play is equally false, when he tells the citizens that, however great their sufferings in the present dearth, they cannot strike against

> the Roman state, whose course will on
> The way it takes, cracking ten thousand curbs
> Of more strong link asunder than can ever
> Appear in your impediment.
>
> (1.1.68–71)

The Roman state, according to this formulation, is not only exclusively patrician, excluding the proletariat, it resembles Coriolanus himself on the field of battle: a titanic machine, its motion timed with dying cries, mowing down every human obstacle in its path.

Of course the city is not the exclusive property of the people, but neither does it belong solely to the upper class.

In the course of the play, Menenius, Cominius, their colleagues in the Senate, even Volumnia, will be forced to recognize that this is so. Although a few young hotheads among the patricians may flatter Coriolanus that he does the "nobler" to tell the mutable, rank-scented meinie just what he thinks of them, how unworthy they are to possess any voice in the government of Rome, although a few may toy with the idea, after his banishment, of abolishing the newly established institution of tribunes, these are not serious or consequential responses. Brutus and Sicinius are scarcely lovable men. There is a world of unsavoury implication in Brutus's reaction to the news of Coriolanus's alliance with the Volscians in act 4: "Would half my wealth / Would buy this for a lie" (4.6.160–61). But they are clearly right in their belief that, once established as consul, Coriolanus would wish to strip from the people the hard-won concessions they have just gained. Such a course of action could only be disastrous. The tribunate, however selfish or inadequate their own performance in the office, is now a political fact. Once granted, however reluctantly, the right of the Roman people not just to rubber-stamp a consular election by exercising their ancient and vulgar prerogative of examining patrician scars in the marketplace, but to make their own needs and wishes felt through their representatives, cannot be withdrawn.

Significantly, in the crisis of act 3, Menenius stops talking about a patrician juggernaut flattening dissenting plebeians like so many weeds. He asks rather that there be "On both sides more respect" (3.1.179), begins to refer to "the whole state" (3.2.34), appeals to "good Sicinius" (3.1.190), "worthy tribunes" (3.1.263), and admits that the division which has cleft the city "must be patch'd / With cloth of any colour" (ll. 250–51). The tribunes, he admits, are the "people's magistrates," and likely to remain so (3.1.200–201). When Sicinius says to him, "Noble Menenius, / Be you then as the people's officer" (3.1.326–27), he accepts the designation without demur, and goes off to plead with Coriolanus to submit himself to judgment. Of course Menenius, like the other patricians, is trying to be tactful and conciliatory in what has suddenly become a desperate situation. Although it amuses him to observe the ebb and flow of popular life in the market, Menenius's basic contempt for the "beastly plebeians," Rome's "rats," her "multiplying spawn," is deep-rooted. Attitudes like these are not changed overnight. Yet he recognizes, like all the patricians except Caius Martius, that a change in the structure of government has become inevitable. Not one of them welcomes the innovation, but they also see that if civil strife is not to "unbuild the city and to lay all flat" (1.196), to "sack great Rome with Romans" (1.313), they have no alternative but to move with the times.

Only Coriolanus refuses to accept that a new stage has been reached in the evolution of Rome. In act 1, he affirmed bluntly that he would rather "the rabble . . . unroof'd the city" (1.1.217) than that any concessions to them should be made. He never relinquishes this opinion. For him, the patrician compromise of act 3, the refusal of the nobles to entertain the prospect of such destruction, take his advice, and try to trample the new power of the tribunes in the dust, constitutes a betrayal both of himself, personally, and of an older Rome to which, in his eyes, only he now remains true. This is why, despite the manifest loyalty and grief of Cominius, Menenius, and the young nobility of Rome, those "friends of noble touch" (4.1.49)—Cominius even tries to accompany him into exile—he can tell Aufidius later that "our dastard nobles" have "all forsook me" (4.5.76–77). Menenius, in act 1, made the mistake of reducing the Roman state to her patrician members. The plebeians, briefly, were persuaded to identify the city with themselves. But only Coriolanus ever deludes himself that he, a single individual, constitutes Rome's best and only self. It is a delusion which manifests itself in the magnificent absurdity of his response to the tribunes' sentence of banishment in act 3—"I banish you!" (3.3.123)—where he effectively tries to exile most of Rome's population, that plebeian majority he detests. Because he thinks in this way, it is possible for him to betray his country without ever admitting to himself that he is, like the petty spy Nicanor, introduced (significantly) just before Coriolanus's arrival at the house of Aufidius in act 4, a Roman traitor.

In a sense, the possibility of such a betrayal has been present throughout Coriolanus's adult life. It is bound up with his essential and crippling solitariness, and also with his failure ever to consider how much his heroism has truly been dedicated to Rome as a city, and how much to his own self-realization and personal fame. Never, it seems, has it occurred to him that the two motives, the public and the private, might under certain circumstances conflict, or that the one might require adjustments and concessions from the other. Of course, he did not mean to be taken literally when he declared of Tullus Aufidius in act 1 that,

> Were half to half the world by th'ears, and he
> Upon my party, I'd revolt to make
> Only my wars with him.
>
> (1.1. 232–34)

The lines are revealing, nonetheless, in the way they elevate a purely personal competition above the claims of a country or a cause. Rome will always need great soldiers, dedicated generals and strong defenders. Livy makes this quite clear. Nonetheless, it is an urban republic, not the plains of Troy, a society which no longer, whatever may have been the case in the past, is based exclusively, or even primarily, upon an ethos of war. One of the great themes running through and unifying Livy's history of Rome is that of the gradual adjustment over the centuries of the claims of peace and war. Numa Pompilius, as the tribune Brutus reminds us in Shakespeare's play (2.3.235–38), was one of Coriolanus's ancestors, that legendary king of Rome who decided in the eighth century B.C. that it was time steps were taken to civilize his people. Accordingly, as Livy writes (in Holland's translation), he began

> by good orders, lawes, and customes, to reedifie as it were that cittie, which before time had been new built by force and armes. Whereunto, he seeing that they might not be brought and framed in time of warre, whose hearts were alreadie by continuall warfare growne wild and savage: and supposing that this fierce people might be made more gentle and tractable through disuse of armes, he therefore built the temple of *Janus* in the nether end of the street of Argilentum, in token both of warre and peace.

Shakespeare could have read about Numa, the great lawgiver and architect of a social and religious order, in Plutarch. There, Numa has a "Life" of his own, paired with that of the Spartan ruler Lycurgus. He is also mentioned in the "Life of Coriolanus." But it is only Livy who patiently teases out the intimate connection, unfolding over a vast stretch of years, between Rome's need to cultivate the arts of peace as well as war, and the internal struggle between her patricians and plebeians. Over and over in the days of the republic, as Livy makes plain, the patricians depended upon war as a way of stifling civic dissension, busying giddy minds with foreign quarrels in order to keep them distracted from injustices and inequalities at home. Sometimes, this strategy worked, uniting Rome temporarily against a foreign foe. But increasingly, over the years, it did not. Rome could not wage war without the help of common soldiers, could not (indeed) even protect her own frontiers. And so, unhappy and mistreated plebeians either declined to enlist or, if impressed, refused once they arrived on the battlefield to fight. It was virtually the only weapon they possessed in their attempt to wrest some rights and privileges from the ruling class.

In Shakespeare's play, Caius Martius appears, significantly, to be the only patrician who still believes that the internal difficulties of the city can be resolved by a Volscian war. The fact that the people are starving need not oblige the patricians to diminish their own stores: "The Volsces have much corn: take these rats thither, / To gnaw their garners" (1.1.248–49). Plutarch, in his "Life of Corio-lanus," describes how at this time the patricians as a group hoped to rid the city of its difficult and seditious elements by way of a military campaign. But, in Shakespeare, it is only Caius Martius who wel-comes war with the Volscians, for its own sake, but also because enforced national service may annihilate "Our musty superfluity" (1.1.225), by which he means the commons, not the stored-up corn. Moreover, Shakespeare altered the order of events as they occur in both Plutarch and Livy. It is plain in *Coriolanus* that only after trib-unes have been granted them do the citizens stop stirring up strife in the city and agree to provide soldiers for the Volscian campaign.

In that campaign, although Coriolanus—not to mention many of the play's critics—later chooses to forget this fact, the plebeians acquit themselves with credit. Cominius is forced initially into an honourable retreat, but he judges that the field has been "well fought" (1.6.1). When, beyond all hope or probability, Coriolanus reappears through those gates of Corioli which he entered by him-self, the soldiers are galvanized into action: they not only rescue him but take the city. Coriolanus could not have done this alone—even though later, just before his death, he seems to think that he did. A thing of blood, looking, as Cominius says, "as he were flay'd" (1.6.22), Caius Martius then becomes a deadly weapon in the hands of common soldiers who, because they possess him, like a living icon of War, become for a crucial moment heroes too. And so the Roman victory is assured.

This is the one instance of real communion and understanding between Coriolanus and the Roman plebeians in the tragedy, but it is ephemeral and special. Upon it, nothing can be built. Later, back in Rome, he will remember only that "being press'd to the war, / Even when the navel of the state was touch'd, / They would not thread the gates" (3.1.121–23). He neglects to remember—even as he neglects to remember the name of the poor citizen of Corioli who once used him "kindly" (1.9.81)—that the common soldiers did in fact enter the gates of Corioli, at the second opportunity, if not, in response to his threats and insults, at the first. Or how men who seemed to him at the time each worth "four Volsces" (1.6.78) caught him up in their arms and cast up their caps in their eagerness for action. The only memory that sticks with Coriolanus is the initial prudence (for him, cowardice) of these soldiers, and the contempt- ible concern of poor men, after the battle is over, for plunder, in the pitiable form of cushions and leaden spoons. A biased, an unfairly selective representation of the campaign, it does nonetheless point to something that is true about the Roman plebeians.

From an early age, as Volumnia tells us, Caius Martius has been dedicated to war, and to achieving excellence in it. It is his metier, his life's work. But the attitude of the Roman people—even, to a large extent, of his fellow patricians—is different. Although the commons can, under exceptional circumstances, be fired with mar- tial enthusiasm, they would really prefer, in Sicinius's words, to be "singing in their shops and going / About their functions friendly" (4.6.8–9). For these small shopkeepers and traders, orange sellers, makers of taps for broaching wine-barrels, military service is some- thing they are obliged to undertake from time to time, when the necessities of the state require it. But they had far rather pursue their normal, peacetime occupations than be out slitting Volscian throats. For Coriolanus, such a preference is contemptible. His view, how- ever, is not endorsed by the play as a whole. The fact is that in an increasingly complex and finely balanced society, one in which even Cominius can hint that valour may not any longer be the chiefest virtue, Volumnia's son is something of an anachronism, out of line even with the other members of his class. Like that dragon to which he likens himself in act 4, and to which Menenius and Aufidius also compare him, he is an archaic, semimythical creature, armour- plated, gigantic, corporeally invincible, a bulwark for the city in war, but something of an embarrassment in peace, because given then to blundering about the market in a bellicose fashion, breathing fire not on Rome's enemies but on the members of her own lower class.

In the second scene of act 3, after Coriolanus has been forced to take refuge from the crowd in his home, Volumnia (who is in large part responsible for her son's scorn of the people, "woollen vassals," as she has taught him to call them, "things created / To buy and sell with groats" (ll. 9–10), and who also recognizes that, as consul, he would quickly show them how he is really "dispos'd" (l. 22), nonetheless begs him now to speak to them not "by th'matter which your heart prompts you," but falsely, in "syllables / Of no allowance to your bosom's truth" (ll. 54–57). The only hypocrisy that Coriolanus manages to utter, before anger and his bosom's truth overtake him, is this:

> Th'honoured gods
> Keep Rome in safety, and the chairs of justice
> Supplied with worthy men, plant love among's,
> Throng our large temples with the shows of peace
> And not our streets with war.
>
> (3.3.33–37)

His sarcasm is barely concealed, but the First Senator responds enthusiastically, "Amen, Amen," and Menenius, "A noble wish" (ll. 37–38). Both of them, unlike Coriolanus, mean what they say. The Rome they want is the one set on its course by Numa: vigilant, strong in its own defence, but also a citadel of justice and religion, and paying equal honour, as befits worshippers in the temple of Janus, to the claims of war and peace. What Coriolanus disdainfully fabricates has become for the rest of the city, including the patricians, a genuine political and social ideal, even if tribunes are now required to help achieve it.

I have been trying to argue that, although Shakespeare is unlikely, while actually writing *Coriolanus,* to have kept a copy of Livy open beside him, as he apparently did with Plutarch, nonetheless the attitudes and interests of *Ab Urbe Condita,* as we understand that work now, live to a striking extent in this last of his Roman plays. But, it might be asked, is it reasonable to assume that Shakespeare in 1607–8 would have read Livy in at all the manner we read him today? As a man of his time, would Shakespeare not have been more likely to value the book for the individual stories embedded in it, for what it had to say about the lives of great men, than for an overall historical view of the kind I have been concerned to stress? Not, I think, necessarily. Here, it seems important to point out that Shakespeare's understanding, in *Coriolanus,* of the development and strengths of the Roman republic, as outlined by Livy, is markedly similar in many ways to that of his great Italian contemporary, Niccolo Machiavelli.

Machiavelli's *Discorsi,* his commentary on the first ten books of Livy, was not published in English until 1636. It circulated widely, however, in Elizabethan and Jacobean England in Italian (a language which, on the evidence of his use of Cinthio for *Othello,* Shakespeare could read) and also in various manuscript translations, three of which survive. The notion that Machiavelli reached sixteenth-century England only as a stock stage villain, a caricature agent of hell, has long since been exploded. Among Shakespeare's contemporaries, Sidney, Spenser, Gabriel Harvey, Nashe, Kyd, Marston, Bacon, Fulke Greville, Ralegh, and Ben Jonson, to name only a few, were clearly familiar not only with the devilish practices and opinions popularly attributed to Machiavelli, but with what he had actually written. Neither then nor, indeed, at any time is a firsthand knowledge of Machiavelli tantamount to approval of what he has to say. The commentary on Livy is morally less outrageous than *Il Principe,* yet even Edward Dacres, its seventeenth-century translator, felt constrained to announce on his title page that he was presenting this work, designed to instruct its dedicatee James, Duke of Lennox in how best to cope with the perils of the political world, fenced round "with some marginall animadversions noting and taxing [the author's] errours." It seems to have been relatively common in Elizabethan and Jacobean England for writers to allude to Machiavelli as a caricature bogeyman or as a serious thinker, according to the needs of any specific occasion. The case of Spenser is especially interesting. In one work, *Mother Hubberds Tale,* it suited him to present the stereotype Machiavel—irreligious, perjured, self-seeking, hypocritical and cruel. But later, in his *View of the Present State of Ireland,* Spenser could, without a flicker of irony, offer Elizabeth's government detailed counsel as to the best way of pacifying that unhappy colony which he took straight out of *The Prince* and, to a lesser extent, the *Discourses.*

I think myself that it would be more surprising if it could be proved that Shakespeare had managed to avoid reading Machiavelli than if concrete evidence were to turn up that he had. Certainly, the example of Spenser ought to caution one against believing that York's reference in *1 Henry VI* to Alanson as "that notorious Machevile" (5.4.74), or the intention of the future Richard III to "set the

themselves early and cannot thereafter be changed. People also, as they mature, learn certain ways of proceeding, accustom themselves to particular patterns of behaviour. States do this too. But around both, times and circumstances change. It is extremely difficult for individuals, and also for political institutions, to vary at need, to accommodate themselves to the demands of new situations. And yet their failure or success depends, ultimately, upon their ability to do so. A republic, Machiavelli suggests in the *Discourses,* is likely to fare better in this respect than a monarchy,

> because shee can better fit her selfe for severall accidents, by reason of the variety of her subjects, that are in her, then can a Prince: for a man that is accustomed to proceed in one manner, never alters, as it is sayd, and must of necessitie, when the times disagree with his waye, goe to wracke.

In effect, once again, the pluralism, the contentious but firmly shared responsibility of the mixed state, work to its advantage.

As might be expected, Machiavelli's view of Coriolanus himself is harsher than Livy's, and much more dismissive than that of Shakespeare. Machiavelli deals with Caius Martius in book 1 of the *Discourses,* in chapter 7, entitled "How useful accusations are in a Republike for the maintenance of liberty." For him, the story of Caius Martius was interesting simply because it displayed the triumph of democratic law. Coriolanus aroused the indignation of a famished populace by declaring in the Senate that corn ought not to be distributed gratis until the people agreed to subject themselves to the nobles and relinquish the tribunate. But the very tribunes Coriolanus wanted to abolish saved his life. If they had not intervened, accused him formally, and summoned him to appear before them and defend himself, he would have been slain in what Machiavelli's seventeenth-century translator calls "a tumult," as he left the Senate. This episode, Machiavelli declares, shows "how fit and useful it is that the commonwealths with their laws give meanes to vent the choler which the universalitie hath conceiv'd against any one citizen. For when they have not these ordinarie meanes, they have recourse to extraordinarie; and out of question these are of worse effect than those." In exiling Coriolanus, and never permitting him to return, the Roman state was guilty of no error or ingratitude, "because he alwayes continued his malicious mind against the people."

It is true in general that "contempt and contumely begets a hatred against those that use it, without any returne of advantage to them." But in a republic, above all, the man who is proud and uses insulting language, who openly displays his contempt for the commons, is intolerable: "for nothing is more odious to the people, especially those that injoy their liberty." There is only one further reference to Coriolanus in the *Discourses,* a passing mention of how his mother persuaded him to turn back from the gates of Rome, used to introduce a debate on the relative merits of a good army or an able commander. Machiavelli does not bother to comment directly on Coriolanus's league with the Volscians. What he thought about it, however, can fairly be deduced from the heading to chapter 47 near the end of book 3: "That a good Citizen for the love of his country ought to forget all private wrongs."

Although Machiavelli took no interest in the nature of Coriolanus's life in exile, Shakespeare did. Caius Martius cannot possibly "banish" the people who have driven him out of the city, restoring Rome to the condition of an ancient, warrior state. On the other hand, I believe, contrary to most critics, that he does find "a world elsewhere" (3.3.135). Historically, the Volscians were a semi-nomadic, cattle-raiding people, hill-dwellers to the south, who envied the rich lands of the Latin campagna. From Livy, Shakespeare would have learned that Rome was at odds with them, off and on, for some two hundred years. She crushed them in the end, but the struggle was long and hard. What seems to have mattered most to Shakespeare, working on hints provided by both Livy and Plutarch, was that in the time of Caius Martius, Volscian society was clearly different and far simpler than that of Rome. According to Plutarch, Corioles was the "principall cittie and of most fame"—modern archaeologists, by the way, still cannot discover where it was—but it clearly had nothing like the centrality and importance for this nation that the seven-hilled city on the Tiber had for the Romans. Antium, indeed, where Tullus Aufidius presides as a kind of feudal lord, seems equally prominent. This is why Shakespeare can so blithely confuse the two places in the final scene. According to Plutarch, Coriolanus was killed in Antium. That is where Shakespeare's scene begins. But by line 90, Antium has turned into Corioli: "Dost thou think," Aufidius exclaims, "I'll grace thee with that robbery, thy stol'n name / Coriolanus, in Corioles?" (5.6.88–90). Shakespeare is being careless, but it is a carelessness made possible by the fact that whereas Rome is unique, one Volscian town looks much like another.

Neither in Antium nor Corioli are there tribunes or aediles. There most certainly is an upper class, designated almost invariably in speech prefixes and in the text as "lords." (Only once, from Aufidius, do we hear the term "senators," 4.5.133.) There are also "people." If there is the slightest friction between the two, we are never told about it. Moreover, in this society, everyone seems to regard war as a natural and even desirable condition of existence. In Shakespeare's play, the Volscians are always the aggressors, never the Romans. According to Plutarch, the Volscian lords were in fact reluctant after the sack of Corioli to break the truce agreed so recently with Rome. They had to be tricked, by Aufidius and Coriolanus, into renewing hostilities. In Livy, it is the Volscian commons, broken and dispirited by plague and by the loss of so many young men in the last war, who need to be deceived into resuming arms. Shakespeare ignored both accounts. When Coriolanus arrives, in act 4, at the house of Aufidius, the Volscian lords have already assembled there to plan a new campaign. While the plebeians, represented here by the servingmen, are overjoyed to hear that there is like to be "a stirring world again" (4.5.225–26). War, they declare, "exceeds peace as far as day does night . . . Peace is a very apoplexy, lethargy; mulled, deaf, sleepy, insensible; a getter of more bastard children than war's a destroyer of men" (ll. 228–32). Moreover, as the First Servingman maintains, "it makes men hate one another." The Third Servingman knows the answer to this apparent paradox: "Reason: because they then less need one another. The wars for my money" (ll. 236–38). In effect, the Volscian plebeians freely accept what in Rome has become a desperate and doubtfully successful patrician strategy: that you can hold a society together, create a bond more important than any social, political or economic inequalities by involving the whole nation in war.

As representatives of the Volscian commons, the three servingmen at Antium do not emerge well from a comparison with their equivalents in Rome. Their behaviour, in fact, on a smaller scale, resembles that of Shakespeare's earlier crowds. Some of the Roman citizens in this play (the Second Citizen in the third scene of act 2, for instance) are slower-witted than others, and likely to be teased about it by their companions. But they are consistently shown as capable of holding an intelligent discussion, and they do not all think alike. The Volscian servingmen, by contrast, constitute a miniature herd. All three of them treat the meanly dressed stranger who has invaded the house with the same high-handed contempt—giving Coriolanus his first taste of what it is like to be thought poor and unimportant. When they discover who he is and how highly their master and the other lords regard him, they swing immediately, and in unison, to the opposite extreme:

> SECOND SERVANT: Nay, I knew by his face that there was something in him. He had, sir, a kind of face, methought—I cannot tell how to term it.
> FIRST SERVANT: He had so, looking as it were—would I were hanged, but I thought there was more in him than I could think.
>
> (4.5.157–62)

The general drift is plain enough, but these men are not very successful at putting their considered opinion of Coriolanus into words. Not, at least, by comparison with the Roman citizens of the first scene, or the two anonymous officers laying cushions in the Capitol in act 2 who can discern both that Caius Martius "hath deserved worthily of his country" and that "to affect the malice and displeasure of the people is as bad as that which he dislikes, to flatter them for their love" (2.2.21–24). When the third Volscian servant tries to impress his companions with a big word, he immediately gets it wrong: "Directitude!," the First Servant asks, "What's that?" (1.215). "Discreditude" seems to have been what his friend was trying to say. Mistaking of words is a common enough lower-class phenomenon in Shakespeare. It does not, however, seem to afflict the citizens of Rome.

Among the Volscians, Coriolanus is universally admired. The common soldiers "use him as the grace 'fore meat, / Their talk at table and their thanks at end" (4.7.3–4). They flock to him, "He is their god," following him

> with no less confidence
> Than boys pursuing summer butterflies,
> Or butchers killing flies.
>
> (4.6.91, 94–96)

This is not the kind of special, momentary blaze of admiration that Coriolanus was able to strike out of Roman soldiers in an extremity, in the heat of battle. In this less complicated, archaic warrior state, it surrounds him every day and it is bestowed by nobles and commons alike. Only Tullus Aufidius resists. A man significantly out of touch with the simplicities of his society, even as Caius Martius was with the comparative sophistication of his, this Volscian lord is reflective and intelligent as his rival is not. Ironically, Aufidius would have found it perfectly easy to be politic in Rome, to "mountebank" the loves of her people, and do all those compromising, diplomatic things at which Coriolanus rebelled. What he cannot do is overcome the Roman hero in a fair fight, and he has apparently tried no fewer than twelve times. His own retainers know this: "here's he that was wont to thwack our general, Caius Martius" (4.5.182–83). Among the Volscians, such physical supremacy counts for much more than it does in Rome. It means that Coriolanus, for the first time in his life, becomes genuinely "popular." It also means that Aufidius, who stumbles on a real truth when he says, "I would I were a Roman, for I cannot, / Being a Volsce, be that I am" (1.10.4–5), who decided after his defeat in act 1 that he could maintain the heroic reputation so important in his society only through guile ("I'll potch at him some way, / Or wrath or craft may get him," ll. 15–16), becomes desperate to destroy his new colleague: a man now worshipped by a nation savagely widowed and unchilded at his hands as he never was in his own country.

"Bring me word thither / How the world goes, that to the pace of it / I may spur on my journey" (1.10.31–33). Those seemingly casual words which Aufidius addresses to a soldier at the end of act 1 are telling. Aufidius is adaptable. Like Machiavelli, he understands the importance of accommodating one's behaviour to the times. He has also divined (as, for that matter, did the Second Citizen in the opening scene) that his rival is fatally inflexible, that he cannot move "from th'casque to th'cushion," cannot "be other than one thing" (4.7.43, 42). In this judgement, Aufidius is almost, if not entirely, right. Coriolanus in exile is a man haunted by what seems to him the enormity of mutability and change. This is the burden of his soliloquy outside Aufidius's house: "O world, thy slippery turns" (4.4.12–26). The commonplaces upon which he broods—dear friends can become foes, former foes, dear friends; it is actually possible to hate what one once loved, love what one hated—have just struck him, as the result of his recent experiences in Rome, with the force of revelation. But fundamentally, nothing has altered in his own nature. Menenius may be puzzled when Coriolanus does not keep his parting promise to write to his family and friends—"Nay, I hear nothing. His mother and his wife / Hear nothing from him" (4.6.18–19)—and initially incredulous that he could have joined with Aufidius. But the Coriolanus who has found a home and adulation among the Volscians remains, in this other country, the man he always was.

Only the embassy of the women can shatter his convictions, force him into a new way of seeing. The scene with the women, outside Rome, when Coriolanus holds his mother by the hand "silent," when he recognizes that he is not, after all, "of stronger earth than others" (5.3.29), has been written about often and well. It is, of course, the moment when Coriolanus finally recognizes his common humanity, the strength of love and family ties. But the victory won here is not, I think, as so often is assumed, that of a private over a public world. Shakespeare is at pains to assert that, in republican Rome, the two are really inseparable. Hence the mute, but important presence of the lady Coriolanus greets as

> The noble sister of Publicola,
> The moon of Rome, chaste as the icicle
> That's curdied by the frost from purest snow
> And hangs on Dian's temple.
>
> (5.3.64–67)

Valeria is a character many critics have felt Shakespeare would have done well to jettison, most especially here. (I have even seen it suggested that the only excuse for her existence in the play is to show us the sort of strong-willed woman Coriolanus ought to have married, if only jealous Volumnia had let him.) But, surely, Valeria accompanies Coriolanus's wife and mother on their mission—even though she is not allowed, as in Plutarch, to initiate it—because Shakespeare meant it to be clear that this is by no means a strictly family affair. Valeria, "greatly honoured and reverenced amonge all the Romaines," as Plutarch puts it, is there to represent all the other women of Rome, those "neighbours" among whom Volumnia, when she believes her plea has been rejected, is prepared (along with Virgilia and the little Caius Martius) to die.

In the triumphal honours accorded the women on their return to Rome, Valeria has her place, reminding us that although the family of Coriolanus have figured as the crucial agents of persuasion, succeeding where Cominius and Menenius failed, ultimately the victory belongs to the city they have placed above family ties, the Rome for which they spoke. Patricians and plebeians, senators and tribunes have already joined together to pray for the success of this embassy. Now, in celebrating that success, Rome is united as never before in the play. Not even Sicinius thinks of anything but of meeting Volumnia, Valeria and Virgilia to "help the joy" (5.4.63). That scene of welcome, with its flower-strewn streets, its sackbuts, psalteries, tabors and fifes, contrasts sharply with its equivalent in Antium/Corioli: the parallel entry of Coriolanus bearing the terms of peace.

We are surprised, surely, to learn from Aufidius that Coriolanus means "t'appear before the people, hoping / To purge himself with words" (5.6.7–8), that there is (as the Third Conspirator fears) some danger that he may "move the people / With what he would say" (ll. 55–56). The Folio stage direction following line 70 of this final scene indicates that Coriolanus enters "with drum and colours, the Commoners being with him." Coriolanus has found it easier to get on with the Volscian commons than with their more pacific but demanding equivalents in Rome. It is striking, nonetheless, that he is prepared now to explain himself and his actions to lords and people alike, that he presents himself initially not as an heroic individual, but as the servant of a common cause: "I am return'd your soldier" (5.6.71). Although he has not been able to make "true wars," he has at least framed a "convenient peace" (5.3.190–91). The attempt fails. Coriolanus tries here to do something which is new to him, but (as Machiavelli knew) the habits of a lifetime cannot be transformed overnight. Aufidius has only to produce that old, inflammatory word "traitor," so effective before on the lips of the tribunes, and Coriolanus is lost. He reacts just as he had done in Rome. And, at last, all the Volscian people remember what, in their adoration of this man, they had been able for a time to forget: the sons and daughters, the fathers and friends he once slaughtered. Here, as Machiavelli would have noted, there are no tribunes to put a brake on their violence as they demand that Coriolanus be torn to pieces, no intervention of law or legal process to thwart the conspirators and enforce a compromise verdict. Coriolanus is simply slain, in "a tumult," while the Volscian lords look helplessly on.

There is a sense in which the characteristically shrewd perception of Aufidius—"So our virtues / Lie in th'interpretation of the time" (4.7.49–50)—might stand as the epigraph for this play as a whole. Whatever the case in the past, or among the Volscians of the present, valour in this Rome is no longer "the chiefest virtue," overriding all the rest. It must, as Coriolanus himself finally discovers, learn to coexist with the values of peace and, even in war, modify its antique, epic character. There is something both touching and full of promise in the prayer Coriolanus offers up in act 5 at his last meeting with his son. He asks that little Martius, the soldier of the next generation, should

> prove
> To shame unvulnerable, and stick i'th'wars
> Like a great sea-mark standing every flaw
> And saving those that eye thee.
>
> (5.3.72–75)

Shame here is more than a strictly military consideration. Coriolanus is thinking of his own, complicated misfortunes, of what may befall a man in peace as well as war. But while the great sea-mark, the lighthouse beacon standing firm in the storm, remains extrahuman, its prime function is not to destroy but heroically preserve. It is an image closer to the one old Nestor finds for Hector on the battlefield in *Troilus and Cressida*—a god "dealing life" (4.5.191)—or to Marcus Curtius dedicating himself to death in the chasm that all of Rome might live, than it is to that of the juggernaut, the mechanical harvester, the Caius Martius who was a savage and undiscriminating agent of death.

Coriolanus is a tragedy in that its protagonist does finally learn certain necessary truths about the world in which he exists, but dies before he has any chance to rebuild his life in accordance with them. Paradoxically, it is only in his belated recognition and acceptance of historical change, of that right of the commons to be taken seriously which the other members of his class in Rome have already conceded, that he achieves genuinely tragic individuality. The play is predominantly a history—indeed, Shakespeare's most political play, the only one specifically about the *polis*. I believe that Livy's account of an evolving republic and also, in all probability, Machiavelli's commentary on *Ab Urbe Condita,* helped to shape it, that although it is certainly a better play than Jonson's *Catiline,* or even his *Sejanus,* it is perhaps more like them in its focus upon Rome herself at a moment of historical transition than is usually thought.

To the question of why Shakespeare should have felt impelled to write such a play at this particular moment, there can be no confident answer. The corn riots in the Midlands and, more especially, the anti-enclosure riots of 1607 which affected his native Warwickshire may well have had something to do with it. It is clear too that there was considerable interest in Jacobean England at this time in classical republicanism, in theories of the mixed state. In his book *Coriolanus in Context,* C. C. Huffman assembles an impressive amount of evidence to show that as James's absolutism declared itself more and more plainly, an educated minority came to believe that the king was trying to tamper with the fundamental nature of English government. England, they argued, was a tripartite state, composed of king, nobles and commons. In it, each element had its rights, with parliament standing as the safeguard against tyranny. James was entirely aware of this line of thought, and of its roots in republican Rome. In 1606, he was fulminating against what he called "tribunes of the people whose mouths could not be stopped"—by which he meant his antagonists in parliament. His concern, and the terms he chose to express it, were prophetic. In the great clash that was to come between king and parliament ("the injustest judgement seate that may be," as James protested) the theory of mixed government was to become a deadly weapon in the hands of the opposition.

Unfortunately, Huffman uses all this historical material to introduce a reading of *Coriolanus* as Shakespeare's apology for Jacobean absolutism, even going so far as to suggest that the dramatist believed Rome would have been better off in ashes, with Volumnia, Virgilia and little Martius dead, than left at the mercy of an institution so wicked as the tribunate. As so often, the settled conviction that Shakespeare's view of history was orthodox, conservative, rooted in the political theories expounded in the Homilies, has blinded the critic to what is actually there on the page. But why should we assume that, in the words of a well-known essay on *Coriolanus* and the Midlands insurrection, "Whether or not Shakespeare had been shocked or alarmed by the 1607 rising is anyone's guess; but it is fairly certain that he must have been hardened and confirmed in what had always been his consistent attitude to the mob"? Assertions like these encouraged Edward Bond to interpret the extremely ambiguous documents relating to the Welcombe enclosures of 1614 entirely to Shakespeare's discredit. One may dislike Bond's *Bingo,* with its portrait of a "corrupt seer," a brutal and reactionary property-owner victimizing the rural poor, but there is a sense in which it simply spells out and exaggerates the received notion about Shakespeare's political attitudes. There is no reason why such a view should persist. Although he remained as fascinated by history as a process in 1607 as he had been in the early 1590s, when he was writing the *Henry VI* plays, the man who conceived *Coriolanus* gives every indication of being more tolerant of the commons than before. He looked attentively at the young Roman republic delineated by Plutarch and by Livy, and chose to emphasize what was hopeful, communal and progressive in it, when writing his interpretation of the time.

Chronology

1564	William Shakespeare born at Stratford-on-Avon to John Shakespeare, a butcher, and Mary Arden. He is baptized on April 26.
1582	Marries Anne Hathaway in November.
1583	Daughter Susanna born, baptized on May 26.
1585	Twins Hamnet and Judith born, baptized on February 2.
1588–90	Sometime during these years, Shakespeare goes to London, without family. First plays performed in London.
1590–92	*The Comedy of Errors,* the three parts of *Henry VI.*
1593–94	Publication of *Venus and Adonis* and *The Rape of Lucrece,* both dedicated to the Earl of Southampton. Shakespeare becomes a sharer in the Lord Chamberlain's company of actors. *The Taming of the Shrew, The Two Gentlemen of Verona, Richard III.*
1595–97	*Romeo and Juliet, Richard II, King John, A Midsummer Night's Dream, Love's Labor's Lost.*
1596	Son Hamnet dies. Grant of arms to father.
1597	*The Merchant of Venice, Henry IV, Part 1.* Purchases New Place in Stratford.
1598–1600	*Henry IV, Part 2, As You Like It, Much Ado about Nothing, Twelfth Night, The Merry Wives of Windsor, Henry V,* and *Julius Caesar.* Moves his company to the new Globe Theatre.
1601	*Hamlet.* Shakespeare's father dies, buried on September 8.
1603	Death of Queen Elizabeth; James VI of Scotland becomes James I of England; Shakespeare's company becomes the King's Men.

1603–4	*All's Well That Ends Well, Measure for Measure, Othello.*
1605–6	*King Lear, Macbeth.*
1607	Marriage of daughter Susanna on June 5.
1607–8	*Timon of Athens, Antony and Cleopatra, Pericles, Coriolanus.*
1608	Shakespeare's mother dies, buried on September 9.
1609	*Cymbeline,* publication of sonnets. Shakespeare's company purchases Blackfriars Theatre.
1610–11	*The Winter's Tale, The Tempest.* Shakespeare retires to Stratford.
1616	Marriage of daughter Judith on February 10. William Shakespeare dies at Stratford on April 23.
1623	Publication of the Folio edition of Shakespeare's plays.

Contributors

HAROLD BLOOM, Sterling Professor of the Humanities at Yale University, is the author of *The Anxiety of Influence, Poetry and Repression,* and many other volumes of literary criticism. His forthcoming study, *Freud: Transference and Authority,* attempts a full-scale reading of all of Freud's major writings. A MacArthur Prize Fellow, he is general editor of five series of literary criticism published by Chelsea House. During 1987–88, he served as Charles Eliot Norton Professor of Poetry at Harvard University.

EUGENE M. WAITH, Professor Emeritus of English at Yale University, is the author of *The Herculean Hero in Marlowe, Chapman, Shakespeare, and Dryden, Patterns of Tragicomedy in Beaumont and Fletcher,* and *Ideas of Greatness: Heroic Drama in England.*

KENNETH BURKE is the author of such crucial works of criticism as *Philosophy of Literary Form, Language as Symbolic Action, A Grammar of Motives, A Rhetoric of Motives,* and *Attitudes towards History.*

NORMAN RABKIN, Professor of English at the University of California, Berkeley, has edited *Approaches to Shakespeare* and is the author of *Shakespeare and the Common Understanding* and *Shakespeare and the Problem of Meaning.*

JANET ADELMAN is Professor of English at the University of California at Berkeley. She is the author of *The Common Liar: An Essay on* Antony and Cleopatra, as well as several articles on Shakespeare and Milton.

A. D. Nuttall is Professor of English at the University of Sussex. His books include *A Common Sky* and *A New Mimesis*.

Stanley Cavell is the Walter M. Cabot Professor of Aesthetics and the General Theory of Value at Harvard University. He is the author of *The Claim of Reason, Must We Mean What We Say?* and *Pursuits of Happiness: The Hollywood Comedy of Remarriage*.

Anne Barton is Professor of English at Cambridge University. She has published extensively on Shakespeare, and is one of the editors of *The Riverside Shakespeare*.

Bibliography

Ansari, A. A. "*Coriolanus:* The Roots of Alienation." *Aligarh Journal of English Studies* 6, no. 1 (1981): 14–34.

Bamber, Linda. *Comic Women, Tragic Men: A Study of Gender and Genre in Shakespeare.* Stanford: Stanford University Press, 1982.

Bayley, John. *Shakespeare and Tragedy.* London: Routledge & Kegan Paul, 1982.

Belsey, Catherine. *The Subject of Tragedy: Identity and Difference in Renaissance Drama.* New York and London: Methuen, 1985.

Berry, Ralph. *Shakespeare and the Awareness of the Audience.* New York: St. Martin's, 1985.

Bradbrook, M. C. *Themes and Conventions of Elizabethan Tragedy.* Cambridge: Cambridge University Press, 1979.

Bradbury, Malcolm, and David Palmer, eds. *Shakespearean Tragedy.* Stratford-upon-Avon Studies 20. New York: Holmes & Meier, 1984.

Brockman, Bennett A., ed. *Shakespeare,* Coriolanus. London: Macmillan, 1977.

Brower, Reuben. *Hero and Saint: Shakespeare and the Graeco-Roman Heroic Tradition.* Oxford: Oxford University Press, 1971.

Bryan, Margaret B. "Volumnia—Matron or Huswife." *Renaissance Papers, 1972,* edited by Dennis G. Donovan and A. Leigh Deneef. The Southeastern Renaissance Conference, 1973.

Bullough, Geoffrey, ed. *Narrative and Dramatic Sources of Shakespeare.* New York: Columbia University Press, 1957.

Bulman, James C. "*Coriolanus* and the Matter of Troy." In *Mirror up to Shakespeare: Essays in Honour of G. R. Hibbard,* edited by J. C. Gray, 242–60. Toronto: University of Toronto Press, 1984.

Butler, F. G. "Vestures and Gestures of Humility: *Coriolanus* Acts II and III." *English Studies in Africa* 25, no. 2 (1982): 79–108.

Cantor, Paul A. *Shakespeare's Rome.* Ithaca: Cornell University Press, 1976.

Chambers, E. K. *The Elizabethan Stage.* Oxford: Clarendon Press, 1923.

Charlton, Henry B. *Shakespeare: Politics and Politicians.* Oxford: Oxford University Press, 1929.

Charney, Maurice. "The Imagery of Food and Eating in *Coriolanus.*" In *Essays in Literary History,* edited by Rudolf Kirk and C. F. Main. New Brunswick, N.J.: Rutgers University Press, 1960.

Danson, Larry. *Tragic Alphabet: Shakespeare's Drama of Language*. New Haven: Yale University Press, 1974.

Debax, Jean-Paul, and Yves Peyré, eds. Coriolan: *Théâtre et politique*. Toulouse: Serv. des Pubs, Univ. de Toulouse-Le Mirail, 1984.

Givan, Christopher. "Shakespeare's *Coriolanus:* The Premature Epitaph and the Butterfly." *Shakespeare Studies* 12 (1979): 143–58.

Goldman, Michael. *Acting and Action in Shakespearean Tragedy*. Princeton: Princeton University Press, 1985.

———. "Characterizing *Coriolanus.*" *Shakespeare Survey* 34 (1981): 73–84.

Granville-Barker, Harley. *Prefaces to Shakespeare:* Coriolanus. Reprint. Newton Abbot, Devon, England: David & Charles, 1982.

Green, David C. *Plutarch Revisited: A Study of Shakespeare's Last Roman Tragedies and Their Source*. Jacobean Drama Studies 1978. Salzburg: Institut für Anglistik & Amerikanistik, Univ. Salzburg, 1979.

Heilman, Robert B., ed. *Shakespeare: The Tragedies: New Perspectives*. Englewood Cliffs, N.J.: Prentice-Hall, 1984.

Heuer, Hermann. "From Plutarch to Shakespeare: A Study of *Coriolanus.*" *Shakespeare Survey* 10 (1957): 50–59.

Holstun, James. "Tragic Superfluity in *Coriolanus.*" *ELH* 50, (1983): 485–507.

Huffman, Clifford C. *Coriolanus in Context*. Lewisburg, Pa.: Bucknell University Press, 1972.

Hunter, G. K. "Shakespeare's Last Tragic Heroes." In *Dramatic Identities and Cultural Tradition: Studies in Shakespeare and His Contemporaries*, 251–69. New York: Barnes & Noble, 1978.

Hutchings, W. "Beast or God: The *Coriolanus* Controversy." *Critical Quarterly* 24, no. 2 (1982): 35–50.

Ingram, R. W. " 'Their Noise Be Our Instruction': Listening to *Titus Andronicus* and *Coriolanus.*" In *Mirror up to Shakespeare: Essays in Honour of G. R. Hibbard*, edited by J. C. Gray, 277–94. Toronto: University of Toronto Press, 1984.

Johnson, Robert C. "Silence and Speech in *Coriolanus.*" *Aligarh Journal of English Studies* 5 (1980): 190–210.

Jorgensen, Paul A. *William Shakespeare: The Tragedies*. Boston: Twayne, 1985.

Kahn, Coppélia. *Man's Estate: Masculine Identity in Shakespeare*. Berkeley: University of California Press, 1981.

Knight, G. Wilson. *The Imperial Theme*. London: Methuen, 1965.

Knights, L. C. *Some Shakespearean Themes*. Stanford: Stanford University Press, 1960.

Levin, Harry. "An Introduction to *Coriolanus.*" In *Shakespeare and the Revolution of the Times: Perspectives and Commentaries*. Oxford: Oxford University Press, 1976.

MacCallum, M. W. *Shakespeare's Roman Plays and Their Background*. London: Macmillan, 1910.

McCanles, Michael. "The Dialectic of Transcendence in *Coriolanus.*" *PMLA* 82 (1967): 44–55.

MacIntyre, Jean. "Words, Acts, and Things: Visual Language in *Coriolanus.*" *English Studies in Canada* 10 (1984): 1–10.

Miller, Anthony. "*Coriolanus:* The Tragedy of *Virtus.*" *Sidney Studies in English* 9 (1983–84): 37–60.

Muir, Kenneth. *Shakespeare's Tragic Sequence.* London: Hutchinson, 1972.

Nuttall, A. D. *A New Mimesis: Shakespeare and the Representation of Reality.* London: Methuen, 1983.

Palmer, John. *Political Characters in Shakespeare.* London: Macmillan, 1945.

Parker, R. B. "*Coriolanus* and 'th'interpretation of the time.'" In *Mirror up to Shakespeare: Essays in Honour of G. R. Hibbard,* edited by J. C. Gray, 261–76. Toronto: University of Toronto Press, 1984.

Paster, Gail Kern. "To Starve with Feeding: The City in *Coriolanus.*" *Shakespeare Studies* 11 (1978): 123–44.

Pechter, Edward. "Shakespeare's Roman Plays as History." *Res Publica Litterarum: Studies in the Classical Tradition* 2 (1979): 55–63.

Pettet, E. C. "*Coriolanus* and the Midlands Insurrection of 1607." *Shakespeare Survey* 3 (1950): 34–42.

Phillips, James E. *Twentieth Century Interpretations of* Coriolanus: *A Collection of Critical Essays.* Englewood Cliffs, N.J.: Prentice-Hall, 1970.

Ribner, Irving. *Patterns in Shakespearean Tragedy.* London: Methuen, 1960.

Rosen, William. *Shakespeare and the Craft of Tragedy.* Cambridge: Harvard University Press, 1960.

Rossiter, A. P. *Angel with Horns: Fifteen Lectures on Shakespeare,* edited by Graham Story. New York: Theatre Arts Books, 1961.

Siegel, Paul. "Shakespeare and the Neo-Chivalric Cult of Honor." *Shakespeare in His Time and Ours.* Notre Dame: University of Notre Dame Press, 1968.

———. *Shakespearean Tragedy and the Elizabethan Compromise.* New York: New York University Press, 1957.

Simmons, J. L. *Shakespeare's Pagan World: The Roman Tragedies.* Charlottesville: University Press of Virginia, 1973.

Stirling, Brents. *The Populace in Shakespeare.* New York: Columbia University Press, 1949.

Stockholder, Katherine. "The Other Coriolanus." *PMLA* 85 (1970): 228–36.

Stoll, Elmer Edgar. *Art and Artifice in Shakespeare: A Study in Dramatic Contrast and Illusion.* New York: Barnes & Noble, 1933.

———. *Shakespeare Studies: Historical and Comparative in Method.* 1927. New York: Frederick Ungar, 1960.

Taylor, Michael. "The Modernity of Shakespeare's *Coriolanus.*" *Studia Anglica Posnaniensia* 16 (1983): 273–89.

———. "Playing the Man He Is: Role-Playing in Shakespeare's *Coriolanus.*" *Ariel* 15, no. 1 (1984): 19–28.

Tennenhouse, Leonard. "*Coriolanus:* History and the Crisis of Semantic Order." *Comparative Drama* 10 (1976): 328–46.

Tillyard, E. M. W. *Shakespeare's History Plays.* 1944. Reprint. Atlantic Highlands, N.J.: Humanities, 1983.

Traversi, Derek. *Shakespeare: The Roman Plays.* Stanford: Stanford University Press, 1963.

Velz, John W. "Cracking Strong Curbs Asunder: Roman Destiny and the Roman Hero in *Coriolanus*." *English Literary Renaissance* 13, no. 1 (1983): 58–69.

Waith, Eugene M. *Ideas of Greatness: Heroic Drama in England*. London: Routledge & Kegan Paul, 1971.

———. "Manhood and Valor in Two Shakespearean Tragedies." *ELH* 17 (1950): 262–73.

Zeeveld, W. Gordon. *The Temper of Shakespeare's Thought*. New Haven: Yale University Press, 1974.

Acknowledgments

"The Herculean Hero" (originally entitled "Shakespeare") by Eugene M. Waith from *The Herculean Hero in Marlowe, Chapman, Shakespeare and Dryden* by Eugene M. Waith, © 1962 by Eugene M. Waith. Reprinted by permission of the author and Columbia University Press.

"*Coriolanus*—and the Delights of Faction" by Kenneth Burke from *Language as Symbolic Action: Essays on Life, Literature, and Method* by Kenneth Burke, © 1986 by the Regents of the University of California. Reprinted by permission of the University of California Press. This essay first appeared in *The Hudson Review* 19, no. 2 (Summer 1966), © 1966 by The Hudson Review, Inc. Reprinted by permission.

"The Polity in *Coriolanus* (originally entitled "The Polity")" by Norman Rabkin from *Shakespeare and the Common Understanding* by Norman Rabkin, © 1967 by Norman Rabkin. Reprinted by permission of the author.

"'Anger's My Meat': Feeding, Dependency, and Aggression in *Coriolanus*" by Janet Adelman from *Shakespeare, Pattern of Excelling Nature*, edited by David Bevington and Jay L. Halio, © 1978 by Associated University Presses, Inc. Reprinted by permission of Associated University Presses, Inc.

"Shakespeare's Imitation of the World" by A. D. Nuttall from *A New Mimesis: Shakespeare and the Representation of Reality* by A. D. Nuttall, © 1983 by A. D. Nutall. Reprinted by permission of the author and Methuen & Co. Ltd.

"*Coriolanus* and Interpretations of Politics: 'Who Does the Wolf Love?'" (originally entitled "*Coriolanus* and Interpretations of Politics ('Who Does the Wolf Love?')" by Stanley Cavell from *Themes Out of School: Effects and Causes* by Stanley Cavell, © 1984 by Stanley Cavell. Reprinted by permission of North Point Press.

"Livy, Machiavelli, and Shakespeare's *Coriolanus*" by Anne Barton from *Shakespeare Survey: An Annual Survey of Shakespearian Study and Production* 38 (1985), © 1985 by Cambridge University Press. Reprinted by permission of Cambridge University Press.

Index